CONDITIONING AND INSTRUMENTAL LEARNING

A PROGRAM FOR SELF-INSTRUCTION

Conditioning and
Instrumental
Learning

A PROGRAM FOR SELF-INSTRUCTION

WENDELL I. SMITH

Chairman, Department of Psychology

J. WILLIAM MOORE

Chairman, Department of Education

Bucknell University

McGRAW-HILL BOOK COMPANY

New York   St. Louis   San Francisco   Toronto   London   Sydney

CONDITIONING AND INSTRUMENTAL LEARNING

A Program for Self-instruction

678910 MUMU 76543210

Preface

The topic of conditioning—both classical and instrumental—continues to be of central importance to psychologists. Hence, it is a topic which deserves a thorough treatment at the undergraduate level—in introductory psychology and in courses in educational psychology, experimental psychology, medical psychology, and the psychology of learning. Since this book has been prepared with these audiences in mind, it includes most of the key concepts and principles in common use in classical conditioning and in instrumental training. Each concept is discussed at the level of the beginning college student; the prerequisite is some knowledge of terms in common use in the behavioral sciences, e.g., stimulus, response, motives, and therapy. Many of the more important concepts such as reinforcement, extinction, and discrimination are discussed more thoroughly than is usual in an introductory text. Further, the humanistic implications of the models of classical conditioning and of instrumental training are presented. Recent developments in interoceptive conditioning and behavior therapy are included to provide an appreciation of the potential value of conditioning models.

We have used this text as a supplement to a leading text in introductory psychology and also as a substitute for the material on conditioning and instrumental learning in the same text. The two uses produced the same level of achievement; therefore, we feel this text may be used as a substitute for the same topics in a standard text.

The authors acknowledge with pleasure the critical comments of Douglas Candland, whose suggestions were invaluable in preparing the final version. We must acknowledge, too, the valuable comments of our students, particularly those of Stephen and Amy Brenner, who spent many hours trying to shape us into better teachers. Finally, we wish to thank Ann Steinbach and Anna Weist for lending their considerable talents to the typing of the manuscript.

Wendell I. Smith

J. William Moore

For the student

This text has several unique features; the authors planned each of these features to make the book a more interesting and a more efficient learning device for the reader. The book may be described as *semiprogramed;* that is, it is a combination of the best features of a text and a learning program. All new information is presented in prose rather than in programed form. Therefore, you can study only the information sections and find all the concepts and principles which constitute the subject matter of the book.

Each information section is followed by a set of items or *frames* which have been programed to serve one of several functions:

1. To teach discriminations among concepts, principles, and viewpoints

2. To call your attention to important material

3. To provide review of information sections

4. To test your knowledge of the material presented in the information sections (Note that the test, or criterion, frames for this purpose have been marked with a ○ before each one.)

The programed sections of this text have been designed to present information in a carefully sequenced, step-by-step (i.e., frame-by-frame) presentation. You should take special care to answer each question—to interact with the material—at least covertly. By responding to each frame, you not only participate in the formulation of the very idea you are studying, but you also have a realistic check on your progress. *If you are unable to answer the criterion frames correctly, be sure to review the preceding prose information section before going on.* The combination of the frames and the prose information sections, then, is an attempt to present the matter of this book in the most stimulating and challenging way possible.

Each frame requires one of several types of responses. Some require that you supply one or more words. For example:

behavior
A ten-month-old child who has just taken his first two or three steps is demonstrating a change in _____.

Some frames require you to select a term from those provided. This is illustrated in the following frame:

responded
The group (responded, did not respond) to the buzzer following the shock.

Still other frames require you to match an appropriate term with a statement.

Three articles from scientific journals have been included in the book. Two of these are reports of research which you will be able to read and understand if you have learned the material that precedes them. The third article, by one of the pioneers in operant learning, presents the author's views on the implications of instrumental training for society. In a sense, the primary purpose of the articles is to provide you with an opportunity to transfer what you have learned to the reading of articles in scientific journals.

Finally, you will notice that exhibits appear periodically in the text. These exhibits are like reference tables in that they isolate and display specific bits of information which help to provide a fuller understanding of what is being discussed.

The authors have found that these features appeal to the students who have used the text. Some students reported that they found this material more suitable to a college audience than other programs which they had used. When they thought they understood the material, they were able to turn to the test frames without reading the teaching frames of the programed portion; at other times, they found the frames a useful means of clarifying the text. The average student found it necessary to read all the material with care. In three groups of students, totaling 120, the average score on the achievement test used was 84 per cent. Fewer than 5 per cent of the students scored below 75 per cent. The approximate reading time for the material ranged from seven to thirteen hours.

In conclusion, the authors urge you to experiment with the various study approaches mentioned above so as to find the one most profitable to you. But they suggest that in most cases you will find you do best by reading all the material in sequence.

13926

CONDITIONING AND INSTRUMENTAL LEARNING

A PROGRAM FOR SELF-INSTRUCTION

Introduction 1

Man's power to change himself, that is, to learn, is perhaps the most impressive thing about him (E. L. Thorndike).

THE STUDY OF LEARNING

From early times, man's conception of himself has included an emphasis on learning as a central process in his behavior, and rightfully so, for learning, perception, motivation, and thinking seem to be the basic processes of behavior. Throughout his history, man has been learning to be human; the recapitulation of this process is easily observable in the first decade or more of the development of any child.

Man's power to change himself is impressive indeed; however, his power to control systematically these changes in himself and others is much weaker. Since learning may be considered a central process in behavior, psychology has been greatly concerned with the discovery and development of a set of principles which will enable man to increase greatly his control of the learning process. Momentary reflection on the significance of the learning process in a technologically advanced society will reveal the challenge which confronts the serious student of the psychology of learning. Directing and facilitating the learning process is at one time or another a concern of practically all adults, since each of us probably will be assigned one or more roles in which this will be a requirement. Parent, educator, advertiser, supervisor, industrial training specialist, politician, minister, public official, businessman, military officer, journalist, and writer readily come to mind as roles in which there is considerable responsibility for influencing what others learn. In a society in which formal education and training have become a lifelong activity for many, it is necessary that society discover the means for directing and facilitating learning. In the United States and in most of Western Europe, this task is appropriately the responsibility of the behavioral sciences and, in particular, of psychology.

THE DEFINITION OF LEARNING

As was indicated in the preceding section, learning is closely related to changes in behavior, although it cannot be equated with *all* changes in behavior. Some changes in behavior are the result of variation in motivational, emotional, perceptual, and physiological states of the organism. The processes of maturation—biological development—produce still other changes in behavior. *Learning,* then, refers to those *changes in behavior* which are a function of *training (experience)* and which cannot be attributed to other processes such as *maturation* and *temporary physiological changes* in the organism. This definition of learning requires an additional qualification, viz., that the changes or modifications of behavior to the stimuli be relatively "permanent" (not transitory).

It is important to remember that as each individual interacts with his environment, maturation and other processes play an important part in his development and in his reactions to and operations upon his environment. However, in man, these processes are greatly overshadowed by what he has gained from previous interactions with the environment, i.e., by what he has gained from experience. As Cole (1953) has written so aptly,

From one point of view, an orderly world has forced man to become reasonable . . . to see and adjust to an order in things. From another point of view man has ordered the world around him, bending it to his will, arranging it in such a fashion that his needs are more completely satisfied.

A puppy that learns to obey its trainer's command to "stay" instead of continuing its playful antics demonstrates a relatively permanent change in behavior. A child who learns to read a simple nursery rhyme is also demonstrating a relatively permanent _____.

change in behavior

In both cases, the relatively _____ change in behavior is a result of training or experience.

permanent

A ten-month-old child who has just taken his first two or three steps is demonstrating a change in _____.

behavior

In this instance, it would be difficult to argue that this change in behavior is a result primarily of _____ or experience; rather, it might be attributed largely to maturation.

training (learning)

Since walking initially is primarily a function of _____ rather than of training or _____, it can be seen that all changes in behavior (are, are not) a result of learning.

maturation
experience
are not

A man who is intoxicated usually exhibits changes in behavior. These temporary physiological changes in behavior (are, are not) a result of learning because they are not dependent on _____ or _____.

are not
training
experience

○ It can be concluded that learning is limited to only those changes in behavior which are a result of _____ or _____ and not a result of _____ or temporary _____ changes in the organism.

training
experience
maturational
physiological

○ Which of the following are changes in behavior as a function of learning and which are due wholly or primarily to other processes? Write either "learning" or "other processes" before each of the following behavioral changes:

other processes	_____1. Contracting the biceps
other processes	_____2. Turning toward the source of a loud noise, e.g., a buzzer
learning	_____3. Eating escargots (snails)
other processes	_____4. A dog's drinking water
learning	_____5. A bird's "talking"

○ Define learning in your own words. Delimit your definition to explaining what learning is and what it is not.

THE LEARNING-PERFORMANCE DISTINCTION

Further refinement of the definition of learning provided in the preceding section is needed to increase the precision with which the concept may be used. An examination of several definitions of learning indicates that the concept covers a rather wide range of activity (see Exhibit 1). As Woodworth (1938) indicates in his definition, learning has many names. Perhaps the concept is defined most adequately by the experiments which have been done under this rubric, as suggested by Hilgard (1951).

Whatever the definition of learning, it must be recognized that the learning process is not directly observable; it is an inference from the behavior or the performance of the organism. In this respect, learning is similar to many other behavioral processes in that the names given to the processes are *labels* for particular classes of responses (performance). In the case of learning, a process in which the stress is placed on *acquisition,* attention is given to systematic changes in a class of responses as a function of stimulation, experience, practice, etc. *The changes in responses do not equal learning; instead, learning is inferred from the modifications which occur.* As we have noted, however, changes in responses also can be attributable to variation in other factors, e.g., motivation, perception, maturation, and temporary

EXHIBIT 1

SOME COMMON DEFINITIONS OF LEARNING

Learning goes by various names: experience, practice, memorizing, conditioning, fixation, or the establishment of a response (Woodworth, 1938, p. 5).

. . . The *inference* to learning is made from changes in performance that are the result of training or experience, as distinguished from changes such as growth or fatigue and from changes attributable to the temporary state of the learner. *The experiments themselves define* the field ostensively (Hilgard, 1951, p. 518, italics added).

. . . A progressive incremental change in the proficiency of performance by an organism; the direction, rate and extent of change in the proficiency of performance are functions of the repetitive or continuous presentation of the conditions under which measurement of the change in performance is made (Brogden, 1951, p. 569).

. . . The ability to combine (or associate) two or more contiguous experiences in cases in which the contiguity is determined by the environment (Maier and Schneirla, 1935, p. 343).

. . . A reorganization of the cognitive field (Kretch and Crutchfield, 1948, p. 112).

Learning can be provisionally defined as a systematic change in response probability . . . in terms of probability relations . . . between operationally defined response classes and operationally defined classes of stimulating situations (Estes, 1959, pp. 395–396).

physiological states. *Only through systematic control of the stimulus conditions is it possible to draw sound inferences about the learning process from an organism's performance.*

One of the difficult aspects of dealing with the concept "learning" is that it is not directly observable. We can observe the performance (behavior) of a dog in response to the command "stay," but we (can, cannot) observe the actual process of _____.

cannot
learning

Since we (can, cannot) observe learning directly, we must infer from the _____ of the organism that learning has occurred.

cannot
performance
(behavior)

If the dog responds appropriately to the command "stay," we _____ from this performance that he has _____.

infer
learned

On the other hand, the occurrence of behavioral changes does not necessarily imply that the organism has learned. For example, one (can, cannot) infer that learning has occurred when the behavior changes following the consumption of alcohol.

cannot

Learning should be _____ from performance only when control is exercised over the relevant *stimulus* conditions.

inferred

A hungry rat depresses a bar to obtain food. The food deprivation is the _____ condition over which an experimenter exercises control.

stimulus

From the preceding illustration, we can only _____ from the _____ (the bar pressing) of the rat that learning has occurred.

infer
performance
(behavior)

○   Under what conditions can we infer from the performance of an organism that learning has taken place?

HABITUATION AND SENSITIZATION

Because the theoretical definitions of behavioral concepts frequently lack the precision of definition found for physical concepts, confusion may arise when one class of responses appears to be so similar to another that accurate categorization is difficult. The modifications in behavior which are called *habituation* and *sensitization* rather than learning serve to illustrate this difficulty.

Habituation

EXHIBIT 2

In the classic study of habituation (Humphrey, 1930), snails were placed on a platform which could be vibrated mechanically. As the snails crawled about, the platform was vibrated at short, regular intervals. This stimulus normally is correlated with withdrawal of the foot; however, after several dozen trials on the apparatus, the snails ceased to withdraw the foot to the vibratory stimulation. Following a period of nonstimulation, recovery of the withdrawal response occurred; however, if further stimulation was provided, fewer trials were required to inhibit foot withdrawal and recovery was less rapid.

The example of habituation given in Exhibit 2 could be multiplied many times over, particularly in lower animals. Careful observation of processes of this type were reported in the literature on animal behavior as early as 1887 (Peckham and Peckham); yet, differentiating the classes of responses of the type exhibited by Humphrey's snails from classes of responses to which the label "learning" properly can be attached is not always easy.

In the experiment cited in Exhibit 2, it was noted that initially a change in the _____ of the snail occurred as a result of a _____ (the vibration of the platform).

performance
(behavior)
stimulus

Initially, this change in performance as a function of controlled stimulation might lead one to

8

learning

temporary
(transitory)

infer that _____ has occurred; however, more detailed examination of the findings
indicates that the change in the snail's response
was only _____.

It was observed that even though the stimulus
conditions were continued, the snail soon
adapted to the conditions and thus (ceased,
continued) to withdraw the foot.

ceased

adaptation
temporary
(transitory)

Adaptation to stimulation is called habituation.
This _____ to a condition is similar to
learning, but the change in performance is only

_____.

performance

stimulus

In this experiment one might have erroneously
inferred that learning had taken place because
initially there was a change in _____
which was a function of a controlled
_____ condition.

habituation
adapted

continued

However, the observed behavior of the snail
might be more properly classified as
_____ because the organism soon
_____ to the stimulus. If learning had
taken place, the snail would have (continued,
discontinued) responding, i.e., withdrawing the
foot in the presence of the stimulus.

stimulus

stimulation

continuous

○ Thus, we can conclude that in both habituation and learning the organism is observed to
make a response as a result of a controlled
_____ condition. However, habituation differs from learning because in learning
the result of _____ is a *continuous*,
systematic change in performance, whereas in
habituation the initial response to stimulation
is soon discontinued in the presence of
_____ stimulation.

Sensitization

When repeated stimulation is provided for any organism, an effect opposite to that for habituation may occur, i.e., the stimulation may result in increased sensitivity rather than in a waning of a response to stimulation. *Sensitization* is a process which is very close to *conditioning* (a form of learning which is discussed in Unit 2), and it is sometimes designated *pseudoconditioning*. Sensitization of the type exemplified in Exhibit 3 has been noted in several species including the human. Because of the close similarity among habituation, sensitization, and simple forms of learning (conditioning), it becomes necessary to use controls for both habituation and sensitization in the design of experiments on conditioning.

EXHIBIT 3

Thirty puppies were divided into two equal groups. Group A received ten applications of shock to the foreleg on five successive days. Group B received ten applications of shock to the foreleg *plus* the sound of a buzzer on five successive days. Before the training was given, no foreleg response to a buzzer occurred in either group; however, following training, the two groups responded similarly to the buzzer, even though for group A there had been no association of shock and buzzer during training. Elimination (extinction) and recovery of the response in the two groups followed identical courses.

An analysis of the experiment presented in Exhibit 3 points out an interesting phenomenon which, like habituation, is similar to _____.   learning

First, it was observed that both of the groups of puppies continued to respond to the _____ condition (shock) over a pe-   stimulus
riod of time (five days). This might suggest that _____ had taken place.   learning

could not

Since the responses of the puppies persisted in the presence of a continuous stimulus, habituation (could, could not) be inferred.

inferred
learned

If one had observed only the second group of puppies (the group which received the buzzer) one might have _____ that the puppies had _____ to respond to the buzzer, because they would exhibit the foreleg response in the presence of the buzzer only.

responded

However, the results of this experiment indicated that group A (the "no-buzzer" group) (responded, did not respond) to the buzzer as a stimulus after having been shocked.

could not

stimulus
had not

It is obvious that we (could, could not) infer that group A had learned to respond to the _____ condition, because the puppies (had, had not) had a previous opportunity to associate the buzzer stimulus with the shock stimulus.

incorrect

stimulus

Since it would be _____ to infer that the buzzer stimulated group A to respond, we can conclude only that the original _____ *sensitized* the puppies in such a way that other stimuli would elicit the same response.

stimuli

sensitization

Thus, the process by which a stimulus leads an organism to respond to other _____ with which they have not had previous experience is sometimes called _____.

sensitization

Because of the similarities between _____ and learning (conditioning) the term "pseudo-conditioning" is often used to describe this phenomenon.

○ Some of the items below are characteristics of learning, some of habituation, and some of sensitization; some may be characteristics of more than one process, and some may be characteristics of none. Label each item appropriately:

_____1. Inferred behavior   learning, habituation, sensitization

_____2. Directly observed behavior   none

_____3. A rather permanent response to a controlled stimulus condition   learning, sensitization

_____4. A temporary change in behavior in the presence of constant stimulation   habituation

_____5. A rather permanent change in behavior associated with a particular set of stimulus conditions   learning

_____6. A rather permanent change in behavior which, after having been associated with a specified stimulus condition, can be elicited by other stimuli with which it has not had previous association   sensitization

HABIT

William James in *The Principles of Psychology* (1890) equated simple learning with habit and referred to habit as "... the enormous fly-wheel of society, its most precious conservative agent." The use of *habit* as a synonym for a stimulus-response unit, an increment of learning, or an association of stimuli or responses has become a common practice among those learning theorists who utilize the model of conditioning in their research (Thorndike, 1898; Watson, 1925; Hull, 1943). Hull, for example, defines habit as roughly equivalent to a "receptor-effector connection." For him, habit is ". . . *a persisting state of the organism* (resulting from reinforcement [reward or punishment]) which is a necessary, but not a sufficient, condition for the evocation of the action in question" (p. 102). The term as defined differs from the everyday usage in which habit is applied to such complex behavior as drinking, smoking, and eating. When habits in the technical sense of learned stimulus-response connections are linked together in several forms, they are referred to as a *habit-family hierarchy*. This concept usually implies the same initial stimulus and the same terminal response, but several alternative habits may intervene between S and R.

habit

Hull (1943) has defined habit as a persisting state of the organism. A rat which always turns a wheel to escape from confinement is displaying a _____ that has been learned.

learned
response (habit)

Since the response of the rat (wheel turning) is a habit which has been _____, it can be assumed that the _____ of wheel turning is the result of previous responses to the wheel.

stimulus

In a technical sense, it may be concluded that habit is the result of learning a relationship between a _____ and a response.

habit-family
hierarchy

It is not uncommon for habits to be linked together. When this situation occurs, they are referred to as a "habit-family hierarchy." Running a maze is an example of a _____.

stimulus-response
relationship

○ William James equated simple learning with habit. What characteristics do these two constructs have in common? _____.

REINFORCEMENT

The concept of reinforcement plays a highly significant role in many of the major learning theories; hence, it is important to much of the research on learning which has been done. The notion that rewards and punishments can be used effectively in the control of behavior must have originated in antiquity; yet, the precise effect of reinforcement in manipulating those classes of responses which fall within the area of learning is still one of the most controversial issues in psychology and is outside the scope of this discussion.

In its general usage, *to reinforce* means to strengthen. In the psychology of learning, *reinforcing* has come to mean *presenting* or *terminating* any stimulus event which will strengthen a class of responses. Any reinforcing stimulus which is *presented* to the organism is a *positive reinforcer,* while any reinforcing stimulus which is *terminated* is a *negative reinforcer.* Whether a stimulus event is reinforcing is an empirical question; if a stimulus event strengthens (increases the probability of) a class of responses or a class of stimulus-response connections by its presentation or by its termination, it is said to be a *reinforcer.*

When food is presented to a hungry chimpanzee each time the chimpanzee responds correctly in solving a problem, it is positively reinforcing if the chimpanzee tends to emit those responses which lead to correct solutions and to cease emitting responses which do not help in finding a solution. Shock, if applied to the foreleg of a dog in association with another stimulus, is negatively reinforcing if its termination leads to an increased probability of foreleg flexion to the other stimulus.

It has been observed that in the process of learning it is possible to increase the probability of a response if the response is reinforced. The food which is given to a hungry rat which has just pressed a lever increases the _____ that it will press the lever again.   probability

In the example above, it is said that the response was _____ by the food and thus was strengthened.   reinforced

A hungry pigeon which has learned that pecking a disk will produce food illustrates the fact that

14

strengthened

a response (disk pecking) will be _____ if reinforced.

strengthened
reinforced

Thus, we could conclude that a class of responses will be _____ if it is _____.

reinforcement
presented to

In the case of the pigeon, the _____ (food) was (presented to, removed from) the organism immediately after it made the response.

presented

In all instances in which the reinforcement is _____ to the organism in association with a response, the condition is called positive

reinforcement

_____.

positive

It would be correct to state that the presentation of any stimulus which strengthens a response is a _____ reinforcer.

stimulus (reinforcer)

On the other hand, a class of responses may be strengthened by the termination of a _____ of a certain type, for example, shock.

presentation

If, then, the _____ of a stimulus which strengthens a response is called a *positive* reinforcer, the termination of a stimulus which strengthens a response would be called a

negative

_____ reinforcer.

positive, negative
strengthen

From these observations, it can be concluded that both _____ and _____ reinforcers _____ responses.

○ What characteristics do positive and negative reinforcers have in common? How do they differ?

_____

○ More generally, it can be stated that reinforcement is:

_____

RESPONDENT BEHAVIOR AND OPERANT BEHAVIOR

In classical behaviorism, it is assumed that a stimulus must precede each response; if there is no stimulus, there will be no response. If one tries to identify the stimulus for each response made by an organism in even the simplest situation, he soon discovers that he has to *assume* the existence of stimuli or to rely on the vague referent, "stimulus situation." Some responses can be closely correlated with the stimuli which precede them; we shall refer to these responses as *respondents* (Skinner, 1953). It is appropriate to state, in these instances, that a stimulus *elicits* or *evokes* the response. In the main, respondents are reflexes: for example, an eyeblink response to a puff of air, a knee-jerk response to a blow on the patellar tendon, constriction of the pupil of the eye in response to light, a salivary response to a food substance placed in the mouth, or withdrawal of the foot in response to application of an electric shock to the sole.

When it can be demonstrated that a response is elicited or evoked by a stimulus, that response belongs to the class "respondents." The class of responses which is not elicited or evoked by stimuli, but which is simply *emitted* by an organism, Skinner called *operant behavior,* which is behavior similar to that which the layman calls "voluntary." The responses in this class operate upon the environment and produce consequences for the organism.

Reinforcement enters into the manipulation of both classes of responses. For respondents, reinforcement is temporally associated or correlated with a stimulus and it *precedes* the response; for operants, on the other hand, the reinforcement *follows* and is *contingent* upon (dependent upon) the response.

In many observations of behavior it is possible to identify the stimulus that evokes a response. When an eyelid blinks to a puff of air, the puff of air is the _____ which evokes the eyeblink.

stimulus

In the illustration, the stimulus which evoked or elicited the response (preceded, followed) the response.

preceded

Any stimulus which _____ or evokes a response must _____ the response.

elicits
precede

If a stimulus evokes a response, it sometimes is possible to use that stimulus as a reinforcer. A shock applied to the sole of the foot may be used as a _____.

reinforcer

The class of behaviors which is elicited by a stimulus is called "respondent behavior." It is assumed that the stimulus which _____ the response must (precede, follow) the response, and that the eliciting stimulus is a _____.

elicits
precede

reinforcer

In addition to the class of behaviors just described, that is, _____ behavior, there is a second class called "operant behavior." Operant behavior is not *elicited* by a stimulus; it is said to be _____ by the organism.

respondent

emitted

If we see a rat press a bar in the course of random movements, we see that the behavior (was, was not) *elicited* by a stimulus; therefore, the response could be said to be _____.

was not
emitted

In operant behavior it cannot be assumed that a
_____ elicits the response; rather, the   stimulus
behavior is _____ by the organism.   emitted

In the case of _____ behavior, as   operant
contrasted with respondent behavior, the reinforcer follows rather than _____ the   precedes
response.

In both respondent and operant behavior, reinforcement is said to increase the probability
of a response in that class. The food that is
given a rat immediately following the pressing
of a bar increases the _____ that it   probability
will make the same _____ again.   response

○ If the following are related to operant behavior, place an O in the space provided; if
they are related to respondent behavior, place
an R in the space:
_____1. A manipulable stimulus is   R
                   used.
_____2. The response is emitted.   O
_____3. The reinforcer follows the   O
                   response.
_____4. The reinforcer precedes the   R
                   response.
_____5. Behavior is controlled by   O
                   the consequences of the act.

Classical Conditioning 2

THE CONDITIONED-EYELID RESPONSE

The eyeblink response is a reflex and, as such, is classified by the layman as involuntary behavior. The blinking of the eye, an example of a respondent, can be evoked or elicited by almost any sudden stimulus, such as intense sound, rapid passage of an object close to the eye, or a puff of air directed against the eyeball. An apparatus can be arranged which will permit an experimenter to present a puff of air of controlled intensity and duration to the eye of a human subject. If the stimulus is administered at regular intervals (once per second), the probability that the stimulus will elicit a response will be very high. Given this environmental arrangement, one now may ask whether it is possible for this response to be elicited by a *neutral stimulus,* i.e., a stimulus which normally or "naturally" does not elicit an eyelid movement. Let us add to our experimental situation a light source from which a small, weak beam of light can be directed to the eyeball. By presenting the light several times, we determine that it does not elicit an eyelid reaction reliably. To ensure greater objectivity in recording the eyelid response, we fasten one end of a thread to a false eyelash attached to the eyelid and the other end to the stylus of a recording drum. A timing device is arranged to control the interval between presentation of the light and the puff of air; a second timer is used to record the interval between presentation of the light and the occurrence of the eyelid response; and a third timer is included to control the interval between trials, that is, between one presentation of the stimulus and the next. Figure 1 shows a similar apparatus for eyeblink conditioning of dogs.

Given this arrangement, we now can begin to answer the question of whether this respondent can be brought under the control of a neutral stimulus, such as light. We may begin by giving repeated presentations of the stimulus light, followed closely by the stimulus puff of air, to each of twenty human subjects. This procedure is followed until the eyelid response is elicited consistently by the light rather than by the puff of air.

A partial outline of a paradigm for *classical conditioning* has been presented in the example above. "Classical conditioning" is the term applied to the model of learning developed and exploited early in the century by the Russian physiologists I. P. Pavlov and V. M. Bekhterev, who, with their students, profoundly influenced psychology the world over. In Pavlov's work, the salivary response was the respondent which was studied intensively; for Bekhterev, motor responses, such as leg flexion, served as the response unit under investigation.

ACQUISITION OF CLASSICAL CONDITIONED RESPONSES

Several significant concepts were derived from Pavlov's and Bekhterev's studies. Each of these is discussed below in terms of the example of eyelid conditioning.

There are certain conditions which are unique to respondent learning. First, the response which is selected for modification has to be a response which is presently in the organism's repertoire. An eyeblink in response to a puff of air and a dog's lifting its foreleg in response to an electric shock are examples of _____ be-   respondent
havior that can be conditioned.

respondent (reflex)

A second requirement is that the response, called a _____ (e.g., an eyeblink), must be elicited reliably by a stimulus. In the case of the eyeblink experiment, a stimulus which reliably produced the response was the

puff of air

_____.

eyeblink

In the example of eyelid conditioning, the respondent is the _____ reflex.

was not

The respondent (that is, the eyeblink) (was, was not) the result of previous learning.

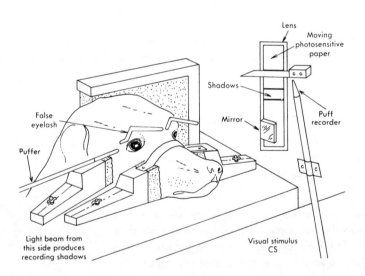

Fig. 1 Eyeblink conditioning apparatus for the dog. Light is reflected off the false eyelashes and appears as shadows on the moving photosensitive paper. The CS and the US also are recorded on the moving paper providing a series of records of the development of a CR. In the record shown here the stages

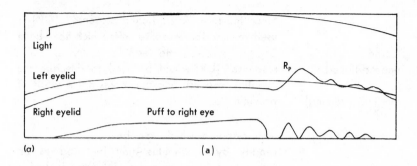

(a)

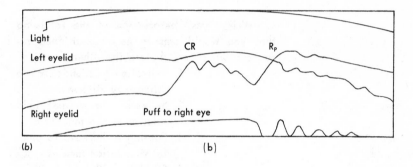

(b)

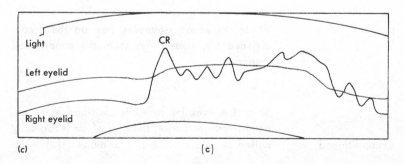

(c)

are (a) a reflex reaction to a puff of air (R_p); (b) a delayed response to light followed by a puff (R_p); and (c) an immediate eyelid response to light in the absence of the puff.

(Redrawn from E. R. Hilgard and D. G. Marquis. Acquisition, extinction, and retention of conditioned lid responses to light in dogs. **J. comp. Psychol.**, 1935, 31, 36.)

Since the term "conditioned response" (CR) is used to describe response units which have been

learned
unconditioned

_____, the term "_____ response" (UR) would be used to describe the eyeblink response because it was not a result of previous _____.

learning (training)

evoked (elicited)

Any response which can be _____ readily by a stimulus may be used as an

unconditioned

_____ response in the Pavlovian model of conditioning.

○ Write "yes" before any of the following that you would classify as unconditioned responses; write "no" before the others.

no

_____1. Salivation to sounds from a laboratory kitchen

yes

_____2. Salivation to a weak acid solution in the mouth

yes

_____3. Foreleg withdrawal to painful stimulation such as shock

no

_____4. Foreleg withdrawal to a buzzer

○ In the above examples, how do the unconditioned responses differ from the conditioned responses?

_____

Since the eyeblink reflex is classified as an unconditioned response, the puff of air is logically

unconditioned

called an _____ stimulus (US).

It was noted in the eyeblink experiment that a

puff of air
unconditioned
response

_____, the US, was capable of eliciting the _____, the eyeblink, without previous training.

A dog lifts its foreleg in response to the ringing
of a bell. The bell in this case (would, would   would not
not) be a US because the response was a result
of previous _____.   training (learning)

O If the statements below are characteristics
of an unconditioned stimulus, write "yes"; otherwise, write "no."

_____1. It elicits a conditioned re-   no
                    sponse.
_____2. It emits an unconditioned   no
                    response.
_____3. It is a result of training.   no
_____4. It elicits an unconditioned   yes
                    response.
_____5. It elicits a response without   yes
                    training.

Any stimulus that does not elicit the respondent
under consideration is called a *neutral* stimulus
for that class of response. A beam of light to
the eye is a _____ stimulus for the   neutral
eyeblink reflex.

Food powder placed in the mouth of a naïve
dog elicits salivation, while the ringing of a bell
does not. Food powder would be classed as a(n)
_____ stimulus, the ringing of the   unconditioned
bell as a(n) _____ stimulus, and   neutral
salivation to food as a(n) _____   unconditioned
response.

If the bell and food powder are paired repeatedly until the bell elicits salivary responses
in the absence of food powder, the bell is no
longer a _____ stimulus because it   neutral
will now _____ a response.   elicit

conditioned
(conditional)

Another name given to a neutral stimulus in the Pavlovian paradigm of conditioning is the _____ stimulus (CS).

conditioned

Once a dog has been conditioned to respond (salivate) to a bell, the salivary response under these conditions would be called a(n) _____ response (CR), rather than a UR.

○ An experiment was conducted in which a mild electric shock was applied to the great toe of a child. It was found that the mild shock elicited a flexion or a contraction of the leg, while the presentation of the spoken command "arc" did not.

unconditioned
stimulus
it will elicit an
unconditioned
response
without training.

1. The electric shock would be classified as a(n) _____, because

_____

neutral stimulus
initially it does not
elicit a flexion
of the leg (i.e.,
it does not elicit
a UR).

2. The command "arc" would be classified as a(n) _____, because

_____

unconditioned
response (UR)
it elicited a
response with-
out training (it
is elicited by
a US).

3. The flexion of the leg to shock would be classified as a(n) _____, because

_____

○ If the command "arc" and the mild shock are paired repeatedly until the verbal command elicits leg flexions in the absence of shock,

1. the leg flexion to the verbal command is called a(n) _____, because

_____

conditioned response

it is a learned reaction (it is elicited by a CS).

2. The command "arc" is called a _____, because

_____

conditioned stimulus (CS)

it is a neutral stimulus which was paired repeatedly with an effective stimulus (it elicits a CR).

PROCEDURES AND TEMPORAL RELATIONS

Merely pairing a neutral and an unconditioned stimulus does not guarantee that conditioning is inevitable. To provide for effective conditioning, a well-controlled, carefully planned situation is necessary. Several of the parameters of the acquisition of a classical conditioned response will be considered briefly to provide some appreciation for and understanding of the model.

Forward conditioning

One set of variables of considerable significance in establishing a conditioned response is the temporal relationship between the conditioned stimulus and the unconditioned stimulus. The most efficient arrangement is to present the CS first, followed closely (for example, less than one-half second later) by the US. This form is called *forward conditioning*. Several variations in presenting the CS and US are possible. The CS can be initiated for a brief duration, and the US can then be initiated and overlap the CS in time. By careful manipulation of the two stimuli, with other factors controlled, an experimenter can determine the duration of the CS and the US as well as the interval of time between their initiation that will result in the most efficient conditioning. According to Pavlov, what is conditioned is the afferent neural state that is present at the time the US is presented.

Simultaneous conditioning

Instead of presenting the CS followed by the US, it is possible to present them at the same time and for approximately the same duration. A CS-US arrangement with a temporal interval of zero seconds is called *simultaneous conditioning*. Generally, no conditioning occurs when the CS-US interval is zero, i.e., strictly simultaneous. At very short intervals such as one-tenth second, acquisition tends to be slower than at somewhat longer intervals such as one-half second (Bitterman, 1965; Kimble, 1961).

Backward conditioning

When the US *precedes* the CS, the procedure is called *backward conditioning*. The research literature provides very little support for the acquisition of CRs when this procedure is used. In the few instances where results were positive, it seems probable that sensitization or pseudoconditioning had occurred.

Delayed conditioning

Given a subject that has had some training and a CS that exceeds ten to fifteen seconds before the onset of the US, it will be observed that at first the CR occurs with the *onset of the CS*. If the experimenter continues to use a CS of this duration, the CR will be *delayed* almost until the *onset of the US*. This procedure was called *delayed conditioning* by Pavlov who demonstrated that delayed CRs could be established with relative ease in the dog.

Trace conditioning

When the CS is terminated *before* the onset of the US, the procedure is referred to as *trace conditioning* ("trace" refers to the aftereffects of the CS on the nervous system of the organism, since the termination of the CS removes it from consideration as the *direct* eliciting stimulus). As a general principle, the longer the interval between the termination of the CS and the onset of the US, the slower the acquisition of the CR. Further, organisms high in the phylogenetic scale can be trace-conditioned more readily than organisms low in the scale; thus, one would expect humans, chimpanzees, and monkeys to acquire trace CRs more readily than would worms, snakes, and fish.

The most efficient temporal arrangement in presenting a conditioned stimulus and an unconditioned stimulus is to present the CS first, followed closely by the US. In conditioning the eyeblink, which stimulus should be presented first— the puff of air or the light? _____   light

In the form of conditioning called "forward conditioning," the US _____ the CS closely in time.   follows

In conditioning an eyeblink to a light, the presentation of the light followed immediately by a puff of air to the eye would be an example of _____ conditioning.   forward

A number of factors may be controlled by the experimenter in forward conditioning. For example, the time interval between the onset of the light (CS) and the presentation of the puff of air (US), and the duration of the CS or the US are important variables. Thus, in forward conditioning, a number of factors such as (1) _____ and (2) _____ may determine the most efficient conditioning procedures.   the interval of time between the CS and the US / the duration of the respective stimuli

A second temporal arrangement called "simultaneous conditioning" presents the CS and US at the same time. Thus, to meet the conditions for simultaneous conditioning of the eyeblink the _____ and the _____   light (CS) / puff of air (US)

28

simultaneously

would need to be presented _____ (with a zero-second interval).

zero

In strict simultaneous conditioning, the rate of acquisition is approximately _____.

backward

In still another situation, the US can be presented before the CS. A procedure in which the US precedes the CS is called _____ conditioning.

○ In the few instances of backward conditioning in which positive results were obtained, it is possible that sensitization occurred. What are the characteristics of an S-R relationship which might suggest that pseudoconditioning has taken place?

_____

○ Each of the descriptions below characterizes one or more types of conditioning: forward, simultaneous, backward, delayed, or trace. Write the appropriate method of conditioning before each one.

delayed, trace
forward
simultaneous
backward
forward, delayed,
   and trace
backward

_____1. Slow rate of acquisition
_____2. Optimal rate of acquisition
_____3. Little or no acquisition
_____4. The US precedes the CS
_____5. The CS precedes the US

_____6. May be explained by sensitization

In forward conditioning it has been noted that if the duration of the CS exceeds ten to fifteen seconds before the presentation of the US, the CR tends to occur just before the onset of the US. If a bell is presented for a twelve-second duration before the presentation of food, it is

0194582

expected that a dog will begin to salivate during the (first, last) few seconds of the bell tone.   last

After several presentations of the bell for a
duration of twelve seconds, the dog *delays* its
response almost to the point when the food is
presented. This form of conditioning is called
_____ conditioning.   delayed

Delayed conditioning differs from forward conditioning in that the _____ is pre-   CS
sented for a duration of ten or more seconds
before the presentation of the _____.   US
If the experimenter continues to use a CS of this
duration, the _____ is delayed almost   CR
until the onset of the _____.   US

The procedure in which the CS is terminated
before the onset of the US is referred to as
"trace conditioning." An experimenter rings a
bell, pauses for a second and then applies a
shock to the foreleg of a dog. Because the
CS is terminated (before, after) the onset   before
of the electric shock, we have an example of
_____ conditioning.   trace

Since the CS in trace conditioning is terminated
before the onset of the _____, it is   US
not the direct eliciting stimulus.

Therefore, trace conditioning refers to the effects of the _____ stimulus in the   conditioned
afferent neural system.

Because the US and CS (do, do not) overlap in   do not
trace conditioning, the longer the interval between the CS and US, the slower is the acquisition of the CR. When a bell is paired with food

30

with an interval of two seconds between the two stimuli

powder, would one expect a dog to learn to respond to the bell more quickly with an interval of two seconds or an interval of five seconds between the two stimuli?

An interesting observation concerning trace conditioning is that the higher the organism on the phylogenetic scale, the more readily it is conditioned. One would expect a fish to be (more readily, less readily) trace-conditioned than a monkey.

less readily

○ Each of the descriptions below characterizes one or more types of conditioning: forward, simultaneous, backward, delayed, or trace. Write the appropriate method of conditioning before each one.

delayed
_____1. The CS is sustained over a long interval of time (ten to fifteen seconds) and the US occurs near the end of the interval.

delayed
_____2. The CR first occurs with the beginning of the CS but after a few trials, it occurs toward the end of the CS.

simultaneous
_____3. The CS and US are presented at the same time for the same duration.

trace
_____4. The US and CS do not overlap.

trace
_____5. The greater the interval between the termination of the CS and the onset of the US, the slower is the acquisition of the CR.

delayed, trace
_____6. Conditioning is noticeably more effective with higher than with lower organisms.

REINFORCEMENT IN CLASSICAL CONDITIONING

Some learning theorists believe that the experimenter must use a reinforcer to change the frequency or the probability of a response in manipulating the class of responses which B. F. Skinner has called respondents. Pavlov conceived of the unconditioned stimulus as a reinforcer or strengthener of the relationship between the CS and the reflex.

The relative effectiveness of the several procedures described in the section on acquisition of classical conditioned responses (pages 25–30) may become clearer by thinking of the US as a reinforcer. In forward conditioning, the neutral stimulus (CS) is presented first, closely followed by the US. In other words, the sequence consists of a brief signal followed by reinforcement (food, sexual contact, water, shock, etc.). In backward conditioning, on the other hand, this sequence is reversed and the onset or presentation of the reinforcement occurs before the onset of the CS. A little thought will show that in backward conditioning, the reinforcement will tend to be associated with those environmental factors which *precede* it rather than with those which follow it, particularly when the reinforcement *terminates a biological drive* or need. In a controlled situation, the stimuli which precede the US in a backward-conditioning procedure are "random" from trial to trial; hence, the organism typically does not acquire a CR to any stimulus which precedes the US in the situation nor does it learn that the stimulus designated as a CS is a signal for reinforcement since the reinforcement has already occurred.

The importance of the *interstimulus interval* (*usually* the time between the onset of the CS and the onset of the US) takes on greater meaning when consideration is given to the unconditioned stimulus as a reinforcer. As a general rule, the longer the delay in providing reinforcement (presenting the US), the slower is the learning. As a consequence, it is to be expected that acquisition would be slower for delayed and trace conditioning than for forward conditioning in which the CS is followed closely in time by the US.

It will be recalled that we have already discussed two types of learning. One was called operant learning and the other was called _____ conditioning.   respondent

follows

precedes

You also recall that in operant learning the reinforcement (precedes, follows) the response, while in respondent conditioning the reinforcement (precedes, follows) the response.

conditioned
unconditioned

In the example of eyelid conditioning, a light was paired with a puff of air. In this example, the light was a(n) _____ stimulus and the puff of air was a(n) _____ stimulus.

elicited

Following several pairings of the light and the puff of air, the light _____ the eye-blink in the absence of the puff of air.

puff of air

It may be said for this example that the _____ *reinforced* the association between the light and the blinking response.

reinforced
(strengthened)

In Pavlov's studies of the salivary response, the meat powder placed in the mouth _____ the association between the bell and the salivary response.

conditioned
unconditioned

In Pavlov's experiment, the bell was the _____ stimulus and the meat powder was the _____ stimulus.

unconditioned
reinforcer

You will note that the meat powder was not only the _____ stimulus, but it also served as the _____ for the association between the CS and the CR.

reinforcer
unconditioned

In the example of conditioned leg flexion to the verbal command "arc," the _____ was mild electric shock which also served as a(n) _____ stimulus.

positive

In Pavlov's work, food powder was a (positive, negative) reinforcer.

The requirement for a stimulus to be a negative reinforcer is that the (presentation, removal) of the stimulus increases the probability of the occurrence of the response.

removal

In classical conditioning, the _____ stimulus is never called a reinforcer, while the _____ stimulus always serves as a reinforcer according to *Pavlov's view.*

conditioned

unconditioned

○ What is the characteristic of a reinforcer?
_____

It increases the probability of a response.

○ What is the difference between positive and negative reinforcers?
_____

positive: presentation of the stimulus
negative: removal of the stimulus

○ When does the reinforcer appear in relation to the response in
1. operant learning?
_____
2. classical conditioning?
_____

after the response
before the response

○ In classical conditioning, which stimulus did Pavlov refer to as the reinforcer? _____
_____

unconditioned stimulus

MEASURES OF THE CLASSICAL CONDITIONED RESPONSE

The dependent variable for classical conditioning, as for other response indicators, must be (1) quantifiable, (2) reliable or consistent, and (3) valid, i.e., a true measure of the class of responses under consideration. The most commonly used measure of a classical CR is *frequency,* that is, the occurrence or nonoccurrence of the response on each conditioning trial. The *strength* of the CR and the *latency of response* are two other measures often used. Strength may mean the amplitude of response where amplitude is measured by an indicator such as the relative movement of a stylus from a base line, the deflection of a needle on a meter, or the amount of salivation. Strength also may be measured by the duration of the response relative to its amplitude, for example, the length of time during which the eyelid responds relative to the amount of response, which is a measure of magnitude (Pennypacker, 1964). Latency of response means the interval of time between the onset of the CS and the occurrence of the response. Other measures of the CR, such as the amount of time or the number of trials required to eliminate it (resistance to extinction) are sometimes used as a measure of strength.

It is important to note that the measures described are not equally reliable and valid indicators of learning. In eyelid conditioning, magnitude is a more reliable and valid measure than is frequency. The response results from the contraction of a sphincter muscle, and frequency as a measure does not reflect the physiological processes underlying the eyelid response as well as does a measure of magnitude (Pennypacker, 1964). Amplitude and latency also appear to be more sensitive measures of the acquisition of the conditioned-eyelid response than is frequency. The important point is that the interrelationship of these several measures of CRs is not perfect; hence, one measure cannot necessarily be used to predict another measure.

The most commonly used measure of a classical CR is *frequency*. If the experimenter observes whether or not the dog salivates on each conditioning trial, the measure of CR used is

frequency   _____.

Although the occurrence or nonoccurrence of the response is an acceptable measure of the dependent variable under some conditions, in the example above one might measure also the

amount   _____ of salivation.

Thus, in classical conditioning we can measure

frequency   not only _____ (whether or not the response occurred), but also the strength or *amplitude* of the conditioned response.

The strength or _____ of a salivary   amplitude
CR may be measured by the _____   amount
of salivation.

One dog salivates (CR) for an average of five
seconds and another dog salivates at the same
rate for two seconds. In this example, strength
may be measured by the _____ of   duration
the response relative to its amplitude. Thus,
magnitude also may be a measure of the
_____ of the CR.   strength

In salivary conditioning, one can measure (1)
whether or not the response occurred, i.e.,
_____; (2) the _____ or   frequency
strength of the CR represented by the amount   amplitude
of saliva emitted; and (3) the length of time a
dog salivated, i.e., the _____ of the   magnitude
CR, a second measure of strength.

A third measure of a classical CR is the interval
of time between the onset of the CS and the
occurrence of the response (latency). A bell
rings (CS)—dog A begins to salivate 1.2
seconds later; dog B begins to salivate 1.4 seconds later. Which dog reflects the greater
latency in responding? _____   dog B

If two dogs received repeated presentations of
a CS in the absence of a US and one dog
ceased to respond after fifty trials while the
other continued to respond for eighty-five trials,
one can say that the second dog exhibited
(greater, less) *resistance to extinction*. Thus,   greater
resistance to _____ can be used as a   extinction
measure of the strength of a CR.

Although it is apparent that a number of measures of CR exist, not all are equally reliable

36

and valid indicators of learning. Because the interrelationship of these several measures of CR is not perfect, one (would, would not) expect one measure necessarily to be a good predictor of another measure.

would not

○ Write the correct measure of a CR before each definition:

amplitude

_____ 1. A quantifiable increase in the acid content of the stomach

resistance to extinction

_____ 2. The number of times the CR occurs after the cessation of the US

frequency

_____ 3. The occurrence or nonoccurrence of the CR

latency

_____ 4. The interval of time between the onset of the CS and the occurrence of the CR

magnitude

_____ 5. The duration of the CR

EXTINCTION

Definition

Returning to the example of eyelid conditioning, and assuming the existence of a CR to a beam of light of low intensity, it is now necessary to consider how one eliminates the habit, in the sense of an S-R connection, which has been established. Must one wait for the habit to drop out of the repertoire from disuse—no practice—or is there a procedure which will result in nonresponse to the light within a brief period?

By returning our subjects to the apparatus after several days of no training and presenting the CS, we determine that the CR is quite stable; it has not simply disappeared, although the strength of the habit probably will not be as great as it was at the end of the last training trial. If we present the CS several times *without* following it with the US, it will be noted that the CR, as measured, becomes weaker and less frequent. If this procedure is continued, eventually the response of the eyelid to the beam of light will cease and *experimental extinction* will have occurred. In effect, *repeated presentations of the CS without the associated US* will lead to extinction. (For an exception to this definition, see the discussion on avoidance conditioning, page 110.)

In an experiment in which a leg flexion was conditioned to a buzzer accompanied by electric shock, the following was observed: after both the electric shock and the buzzer were discontinued for a period of time, the presentation of the buzzer alone would elicit the response. The buzzer continued to function as a _____ stimulus.

conditioned

After repeated presentations of the buzzer alone, the leg ceased to respond. From this observation, it can be concluded that the CS will cease to elicit the CR if the CS is presented repeatedly in the absence of the _____.

US

We may conclude that repeated presentations of the _____ stimulus in the absence of the _____ stimulus will lead to nonresponse to the _____ stimulus.

conditioned
unconditioned
conditioned

This is called "experimental extinction," and the response is said to have been _____.

extinguished

○ What is the relationship between the CS and the US when extinction takes place?

Spontaneous recovery

Experimental extinction should not be equated with *forgetting,* if the term "forgetting" implies a complete loss of habit. If we return our subjects, whose conditioned-eyelid responses have been extinguished, to the experimental environment an hour or two *after extinction has first occurred* and present the beam of light, we shall discover that the eyeblink response occurs again. This process is called *spontaneous recovery*. During the period of rest, the probability of a response has increased, although not to the level of strength attained on the first extinction trial. Recovery of response strength is incomplete, reaching approximately 50 per cent of its original level. If we extinguish the response again, permit the subjects to rest, and then return them to the apparatus, we may find that several subjects respond to the CS once again, i.e., that recovery of response strength of the CR is high. Several periods of extinction may be required before the loss of the habit *approaches* an absolute. Absolute loss of a habit is infrequent.

This brief discussion of spontaneous recovery has dealt with the concept in an idealized manner. The rate and amount of recovery are affected significantly by the procedures followed in acquiring and extinguishing the CR, that is, by whether trials are massed or spaced and whether extinction trials are continued well beyond the point of nonresponse. Further, whether the conditioning was accomplished with positive or with negative reinforcers has been found to be an important variable in extinction and in recovery from extinction.

If many extinction trials are given over a long period of time, the CS actually inhibits acquisition when reconditioning to the same CS is attempted. Pavlov aptly called this phenomenon "extinction below zero," i.e., below the base line of the response to the US. It is probable that both age and species differences would affect rate of extinction and the amount of spontaneous recovery.

should not	Experimental extinction (should, should not) be equated with forgetting, if forgetting implies an absolute loss of a habit.
forgetting	Experimental extinction appears to have the same characteristics as _____; however, since the response may recur following a period of rest, it is apparent that during a period of rest the probability of a response may
increase	(increase, decrease).

Spontaneous recovery, the recovery of a response following extinction, is usually incomplete—rarely above 50 per cent. You should not be surprised to observe that the strength of a CR following extinction is weaker than it was preceding extinction. The recovery of an extinguished CR following a period of rest is called _____.

spontaneous recovery

If one wished to reduce the frequency of a CR to zero, one would (increase, decrease) the number of extinction trials.

increase

Spontaneous recovery is affected by the strength of the CR. If learning trials are spaced rather than massed, one would expect more _____.

spontaneous recovery

In addition to being affected by the _____ of the CR, spontaneous recovery is also affected when trials are continued well beyond the point of nonresponse. In this case, the amount of spontaneous recovery is (increased, decreased).

strength

decreased

One would expect the probability of spontaneous recovery to be (greater, less) after 14 extinction trials after the organism ceases to respond than after 50 extinction trials after nonresponse.

greater

If many extinction trials are given over a long period of time, the CS may become inhibitory (extinction below zero may occur). Under these conditions, the probability of a response to the CS is (greater, less) than it was prior to conditioning.

less

○ How does extinction differ from forgetting?

_____

○ Identify three or more factors which affect spontaneous recovery.

    1. _____

    2. _____

    3. _____

○ What is meant by extinction below zero?

_____

How is it brought about?

_____

External inhibition

If in the course of the acquisition of a conditioned response, a neutral or novel stimulus is introduced in association with the CS, what will be the organism's reaction? Pavlov found that a novel stimulus has *inhibitory* properties; thus, the CR is reduced in strength or it is not made at all on that trial. In eyelid conditioning to a beam of light, for example, the presentation of a sharp clicking sound preceding the presentation of light would reduce the probability of an eyelid response on that trial. Pavlov called this effect of novel stimuli *external inhibition*.

Disinhibition

If in the course of the *extinction* of a conditioned response, a neutral or novel stimulus is introduced in association with the CS, will it produce the same effects as were described for acquisition? Pavlov found that the answer to this question was "no." If a CS of light is preceded by a sharp click during the extinction trials in eyelid conditioning, the novel stimulus will *increase* the probability or strength of a response, that is, the clicking sound will release or *disinhibit* the response.

External inhibition and disinhibition are important phenomena in Pavlov's theory of the central nervous processes underlying conditioning; however, a discussion of this theory is delayed until three other phenomena are considered. It is clear from the studies of inhibitory effects of extraneous or novel stimulation that the conditioning procedure is affected significantly by the context in which the CS is presented.

Pavlov observed that a novel stimulus has inhibitory properties. For example, in eyelid conditioning the presentation of a sharp click preceding the presentation of the CS (increases, reduces) the probability of an eyelid response on that trial.

reduces

The _____ stimulus has inhibitory properties if introduced during the acquisition of a CR.

novel

The _____ effect of the novel stimulus on the CR is called external inhibition.

inhibitory

If the introduction of a novel stimulus during the *acquisition* of a CR reduces the probability that the CR will occur, then one would expect that the introduction of a novel stimulus during the *extinction* of a CR would (increase, reduce) the probability that the CR will occur.

increase

If the novel stimulus increases the probability of the CR, it can be assumed that the organism is in the process of _____ the conditioned response, whereas if the novel stimulus decreases the probability that the CR will occur, it can be assumed that the organism is in the process of _____ the CR.

extinguishing

acquiring

When a novel stimulus increases the probability of a response during the course of extinction, the stimulus _____ the CR.

disinhibits

○ A dog is in the process of being conditioned to flex his leg in response to a buzzer. A bright light is presented preceding the CS.

1. What effect would you expect the introduction of the light to have on the foot-lifting response?

It would inhibit it.

external inhibition _____

It would increase 2. This effect is called _____.
the probability 3. If the conditions are the same with the
of the occur- exception that the leg flexion is being ex-
rence of the tinguished, what would be the effect of the light?
response.

_____

disinhibition 4. What is this effect called? _____

GENERALIZATION

If the intensity of the beam of light which is used as a CS in eyelid conditioning is varied over a wide range after a stable CR has been established, it will be noted that the CR was established to a *class* of stimuli, not to a single stimulus, i.e., not to a beam of light of a specific intensity. The process described is called *stimulus generalization* and it is an important property of learning. In effect, an organism learns to respond initially to a class of related stimuli rather than to a single stimulus; however, it does not necessarily respond to all elements of the class, nor are the responses which are given necessarily all of equal strength. Generally it can be said that response strength will vary over the range of stimuli of the class from zero at the extremes of the range to a maximum at the point in the class at which the CS is located. The spread or range of effective stimuli is referred to as a *generalization gradient.*

Generalization from conditioning can occur for *responses* as well as for stimuli. Kellogg (1939) found that a CR of leg flexion in response to a buzzer generalized to all three of the other legs even though none of the three ever received shock. *Response generalization* presumably exhibits a *gradient,* although it is difficult at this stage of development for experimenters to demonstrate the gradient because of the difficulty of classifying responses quantitatively. Kellogg's dogs probably were exhibiting a response-generalization gradient of a crude nature.

When an organism which has been conditioned
to respond to one stimulus responds to other
stimuli within that class without specific training, stimulus generalization is said to have occurred. A bird is conditioned to peck a blue
disk. Upon the presentation of a green disk,
the bird pecks it also. This is an example of   stimulus
_____.   generalization

One would not expect the strength of the responses to be the same for all stimuli within a
class. If the bird is conditioned to respond to a
CS of 500 cycles per second, a stimulus of (600
cps, 100 cps) is likely to produce the stronger   600 cps
response.

Just as the generalization of a conditioned
stimulus is called _____ generaliza-   stimulus
tion, the generalization of a CR is called
_____ generalization. The finding   response
that a CR of leg flexion in response to a buzzer
generalized to the other three legs, even though
none of the three ever received shock, is an   response
example of _____.   generalization

○ An infant is conditioned to smile to the
verbal stimulus "pretty." It is found that the
infant also will smile to the verbal stimulus
"silly" even though "silly" had not been paired
previously with a US. This is an example of   stimulus
_____.   generalization

○ A CR made in response to a stimulus without training is an example of _____   response
generalization.

CONDITIONED DISCRIMINATION

In the preceding section, it was noted that stimulus generalization is
an important characteristic of learning. However, it may occur to the

reader that even though making the same response to a broad range of similar stimuli may be efficient, there are many times when adaptation would call for a discrimination or differentiation among similar stimuli. For example, we used a beam of white light of low intensity as a CS in conditioning the eyelid response. The CR was elicited by a range of stimulus intensities. We may assume that several colors of light other than white also would elicit the CR as a result of stimulus generalization. If we find that a red light and a yellow light of equal intensity are capable of eliciting an eyelid response, we may ask whether it is possible for the organism to be trained to respond to the red light but not to the yellow, that is, whether we can train for *differentiation* between stimuli.

If the red light (CS_1), followed by the puff of air, is presented repeatedly, while on alternate blocks of trials the yellow light (CS_2) is presented *in the absence of* the puff of air, the response to the red light will continue while the response to the yellow light will extinguish, assuming that the organism is able to discriminate red from yellow. Thus, through a process of *differential inhibition,* a discrimination will be taught. Lights of other colors may be rendered neutral by extinguishing CRs to them through repeated presentations of these stimuli in the absence of the puff of air.

The technique of differential conditioning or conditioned discrimination is useful in testing the sensory capacities and the discriminative abilities of a wide range of species, including man.

generalization

In an experiment it was observed that a tactual stimulus (CS_1) applied to a dog's right side and followed by shock to his leg conditioned the dog to flex his leg to a tactual stimulus applied to *either* his right or left side (CS_2). This is an example of stimulus _____.

continue

To teach the dog to discriminate between CS_1 and CS_2, CS_1 and shock were presented for several trials. One would expect the flexion of the leg to (continue, cease).

In alternate blocks of trials, CS_2 (tactual stimulus to the right side) was presented in the

absence of the shock. After a period of time the
flexion of the leg ceased. The response to the
CS$_2$ had _____.   extinguished

Thus, we can teach an animal to discriminate by
providing conditions which will lead it to *inhibit*
a response to all stimuli except the CS$_1$. In the
illustration, only responses to CS$_2$ were extinguished. Thus, a discrimination was taught
through a process of differential _____.   inhibition

○ When an organism responds to only one CS
of a class of stimuli, all of which previously
evoked the same response, the organism has
learned to _____.   discriminate

○ The process of learning to discriminate be-   differential
tween stimuli is called _____.   inhibition

○ In the process, all stimuli except CS$_1$ are
rendered neutral by _____ responses   extinguishing
to them.

HIGHER-ORDER CONDITIONING

One may ask whether conditioned responses are formed only when a
CS is accompanied by a US such as electric shock or meat powder.
If so, the conditioning paradigm can account for little of the learning
which takes place in animals and man, since many habits seem to be
formed in the absence of a "natural" stimulus, a primary US. Pavlov
found that CSs may be formed using any stimulus for which the
probability of eliciting a response approaches unity, that is, 1.00.
*Thus, one should be able to use a former CS as a US once a stable
CR has been established.*

Given a stable eyelid response to a beam of light, a stimulus which
will elicit the response on practically all the trials, one now can use
the beam of light as an *unconditioned* stimulus. If the click of a
metronome is used as a new CS for eyelid conditioning closely followed by the beam of light, the eyeblink response will be "trans-

ferred" to the click following many paired presentations. This procedure was called *higher-order conditioning* by Pavlov, who succeeded in demonstrating that three orders of conditioned responses could be established in his subjects. In the example in which the click and the light were paired, a *second-order* conditioned response was described. Theoretically, once the click comes to elicit an eyelid response regularly, it could be used as a US to form a *third-order* conditioned response. Thus, it might be expected that if a tactual stimulus (a new CS) was paired repeatedly with the click, the tactual stimulus would become a substitute or signal for the click, which would be a substitute or signal for a light, which in turn would be a substitute or signal for a puff of air. In practice, stable third-order conditioned responses are difficult to establish in the laboratory.

The difficulty which one faces in establishing higher-order conditioned responses arises from the process of extinction. It will be recalled that repeated presentation of the CS in the absence of the US eventually results in extinction. Thus, it has been found that presenting the light on trial after trial in the absence of a puff of air eventually will lead to extinguishing the eyelid response to light. In training for second-order CRs, the experimenter tries to prevent extinction by retraining his subjects in the *first-order* CS whenever the response measure indicates that some extinction is occurring. In training for third-order CRs, the experimenter will have to retrain his subjects on both the first- *and* the second-order CRs periodically; otherwise, extinction will take place and the US which he is using to establish the third order will cease to elicit the desired response.

In summary, it is possible to demonstrate that the conditioning paradigm is capable of handling some situations in which a habit is acquired in the absence of a primary stimulus, that is, a stimulus which characteristically elicits a response in the species under consideration.

higher-order	In the previous discussion, it was noted that the procedure of using a stable CS as a US in establishing a new CR was called _____ conditioning by Pavlov.

One of the criteria to be met for a CS to be used as a US is that the CS must elicit a re-

sponse almost _____ per cent of the   100
time.

Complete the following:
US\
  | CR₁ (first order)   ⎺|⎺\CR₂ (second order)   CS₁
CS/   CS₂/

Complete the following
?\   CS₂
 ⎺\CR₃   _____ order response   CS₃
?/   third-

If extinction begins to occur on CR₂, retraining
will be required on _____. If extinc-   CR₁
tion begins to occur on CR₃, retraining will
be required on both _____ and   CR₂
_____.   CR₁

○ What is higher-order conditioning?   using a former
_____   CS as a US

○ Complete the following:
US\
   \CR₁ (first-order CR)
CS/

?\
⎺\ ? (second-order CR)
?/

?\
⎺\ ? (third-order CR)
?/

CLASSICAL CONDITIONING AND THE PLANARIAN

The article which follows has been included to provide the reader
with an example of current research in which several of the concepts
used in classical conditioning are discussed. The evidence for the
conditioning of the planarian, a flatworm, has provoked controversy

over whether learning occurs in a simple organism of this type or whether only sensitization is demonstrated.

Conditioned discrimination in the planarian*

Abstract. To demonstrate classical conditioning in the planarian in a situation uncontaminated by the possible artifacts of pseudoconditioning or sensitization 30 *Phagocata gracilis* were successfully trained, by the use of directional shock as the unconditioned stimulus, to turn in one direction to a light, and in the opposite direction to vibration. Ten similarly trained planaria tested by an independent observer who did not know the previous training conditions experienced by any animal showed similar results.

Thompson and McConnell's report of classical conditioning in the planarian (1) has revived interest in the learning abilities of this primitive organism. The literature has been reviewed recently by Jacobson (2). However, there has been concern with the possibility that much, or all, of the evidence for classical conditioning in the planarian might really be an artifact of the experimental situation. A basic source of possible artifact lies in the tendency of a response which has been repeatedly elicited to become "dominant," or more probable of occurrence (3). If the response is one elicited by the unconditioned stimulus (UCS), the tendency to make this same response to any other stimulus, in the absence of associative pairing, has been termed pseudoconditioning. Moreover, if the response is one directly (innately) elicited by the conditioned stimulus (CS), the increased probability of response has been called sensitization (3), and is of concern here because the light used as a CS by Thompson and McConnell can, innately, elicit the criterion response of contraction or turning. In addition to their classical conditioning group, Thompson and McConnell ran control groups which were exposed, respectively, only to the CS, only the UCS (electric shock), and to no stimulation whatever. Neither the CS-only nor the UCS-only group showed ultimate response levels significantly higher than that of the no-stimulation group. On the other hand, Halas, James, and Knutson (4) found that a CS-only group, in a situation similar to Thompson and

* Griffard, C. D., and Pierce, J. T., in *Science,* 1964, **144,** 1472–1473. (Copyright 1964 by the American Association for the Advancement of Science.) Reprinted with the permission of the authors and the publisher from the article of the same title.

McConnell's, did give significantly more responses than a no-stimulation control.

We were interested in showing classical conditioning in a situation where there could be no question of artifactual "conditioning" due to sensitization or pseudoconditioning. Exploiting the planarian's marked galvanotropism, we were able to concurrently condition homologous, mutually exclusive responses to two different CS's and thus not only demonstrate conditioning but also test the planarian's ability to form a conditioned discrimination.

The subjects were 30 large *Phagocata gracilis*, obtained as needed during the study from a local stream. All were run within 24 hours of capture.

A plastic petri dish, 8.8 cm in diameter by 2.5 cm deep, filled to a depth of 2 cm with aged tap water, constituted the experimental chamber. A white base, with a reference grid to aid in evaluating the response, was glued to the underside of the chamber. This assembly was then firmly secured to the cover of a Johnson Speed-X constant-frequency buzzer, the vibration from which served as one CS. A commutator, 12.5 cm above the chamber, supported both a clear 12-watt light, which served as the second CS, and two nonpolarizing, platinum electrodes which extended down into the water on opposite sides of the chamber. By rotating the commutator, the electrodes could be oriented across any diameter of the chamber. The UCS, electric shock, was supplied by a filtered 8.5-volt d-c power supply in series with a variable resistance and a milliameter. Since the planaria showed differential sensitivity to the UCS, the current was individually adjusted during the

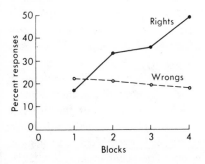

Percentage of correct and incorrect test-trial responses (of amplitude greater than 22.5 degrees) in successive blocks of 50 training trials.

first few trials to the minimum level required to evoke a vigorous response. Most subjects required between 1.7 and 2.2 milliamperes.

All the planaria were trained and tested individually, receiving 200 training trials divided into four blocks of 50 training trials each. Ten test trials were given per block, five for each CS. The sequence both of training and of test CS presentation was randomly, though separately, determined. Test trials were given after each five training trials. The average intertrial interval was about 18 seconds, and rest periods of 1 to 2 hours were given between blocks of trials. During rest periods, the planaria were kept in individual containers in a dark room.

Each training trial consisted of a 3-second presentation of one or the other CS, with the UCS starting approximately 0.5 second after the onset of the CS and terminating with the termination of the CS. A test trial consisted of a 3-second presentation of one or the other CS alone.

By rotating the commutator so that the anodal electrode was in a position about 25 to 30 degrees to one or the other side of the subject's line of travel, either a right- or a left-turning unconditioned response could be elicited, the direction of the turn being away from the anode. As the animal started to turn at the onset of shock, the electrodes were rotated, "tracking" the animal and forcing a turn of more than 90 degrees. Half the subjects were run with the light paired with right turning and the buzzer with left turning, the other half with the reverse arrangement.

Responses were recorded in terms of both direction and amplitude of turn. No test trial was given until the animal was gliding in a straight line. In cases where it turned first in one direction, then in the other, only the initial direction and magnitude were recorded. A score of 0 was entered on trials where the animal did not turn or where the turn was judged as being less than 22.5 degrees, since planaria frequently make small turning motions of the head during normal locomotion. The measure for each subject, then, consisted of the number of correct and incorrect responses judged to be greater than 22.5 degrees. These data were used as the cell entries in a 30 (subjects) × 4 (blocks of trials) × 2 (right-wrong) × 2 (light-vibration) design. By means of the analysis of variance, tests of significance were made for each of the main effects and for each of the possible interactions. A summary of this analysis appears in Table 1. Both the blocks main effect (B) and the right-wrong (RW) main effect were significant at the .001 level. Most important is the B × RW interaction, which was also significant at the .001 level. [The graph on page 49] shows that this interaction was due to an increasing number of correct responses and a decreasing number of

Table I. Summary of Analysis of Variance for Responses of 30 Planaria to Two Conditioned Stimuli (Light and Vibration).

Source	df	Sum of squares	Mean square	F	p
Subjects (Ss)	29	85.84			
Blocks of trials (B)	3	26.19	8.73	11.60	< .01
Right-wrong (RW)	1	57.41	57.41	35.22	< .01
Light-vibration (LV)	1	1.41	1.41	1.32	> .05
B × RW	3	49.87	16.62	12.49	< .01
B × LV	3	1.97	0.66	1.08	> .05
RW × LV	1	7.50	7.50	3.15	> .05
B × RW × LV	3	9.15	3.05	2.44	> .05
B × Ss	87	65.44	0.752		
RW × Ss	29	47.22	1.63		
LV × Ss	29	31.22	1.07		
B × RW × Ss	87	116.00	1.33		
B × LV × Ss	87	54.90	0.63		
RW × LV × Ss	29	68.87	2.37		
B × RW × LV × Ss	87	108.98	1.25		

incorrect responses from one block of trials to the next. This is, of course, our indication of learning.

While an additional test indicated individual differences in right-turning and left-turning tendencies, a separate analysis showed that the probability of a correct response on a test trial was not significantly affected by whether the preceding trial had been with the same CS as that used in the test trial or with the alternate.

As a check on possible experimenter bias in recording responses, 10 additional planaria were run under the same conditions as the original 30 except that all test-trial responses were scored by an independent observer, who observed only the test trials and was unaware of what constituted a correct or incorrect response for any subject. Group curves for these subjects were virtually identical to those shown in [the graph], and similar, statistically significant evidence of learning was obtained.

We believe that these data give less equivocal evidence of classical conditioning in the planarian than have any previously reported. In earlier studies, the only measure taken was whether the subject did or did not respond on a given test trial. By conditioning two distinct and homologous responses to the two different CS's, we are in a position to measure learning in terms of both correct and incorrect responses, rather than simply measure the total number of responses. Though it is possible that the subjects of this study became somewhat sensitized or pseudoconditioned to the experimental stimuli, neither sensitization nor pseudoconditioning can account for the increasing divergence in number of the correct and the incorrect responses, since there is no way these can differentially affect the responses to the two CS's, and since an equal number of unconditioned turns had been made to each side.

To the extent that other species of planaria have similar learning capacities, it seems likely that Thompson and McConnell's subjects did develop a simple conditioned response. The development of a conditioned discrimination by the subjects of this study suggests the need for further research concerning the limits of learning in this primitive organism.

References

1. **Thompson, R., and McConnell, J. V.** *J. Comp. Physiol. Psychol.,* 1955, **48,** 65.
2. **Jacobson, A. L.** *Psychol. Bull.,* 1962, **60,** 74.
3. **Kimble, G. A.** (rev.). *Hilgard and Marquis' Conditioning and Learning* (2d ed.) New York: Appleton-Century-Crofts, 1961.
4. **Halas, E. S., James, R. L., and Knutson, C. S.** *J. Comp. Physiol. Psychol.,* 1962, **55,** 969.

INTEROCEPTIVE CONDITIONING

Several generations of American college students have learned about the model of classical conditioning based on Pavlov's work; however, few students have ever been helped to see the significance of the model. Conditioning the salivary response, leg flexion, or the eyeblink to a range of stimuli seemed to be little more than an interesting demonstration—a special case—of associative learning. In fact, until recently few American psychologists have been interested in extending significantly the work of Pavlov, Bekhterev, and their students. Largely through the efforts of one American psychologist, Gregory Razran, several reports of the Russian work on classical conditioning during the last two decades have been published. Because of the potential value of the Russian work to such important problems as psychopathology, mental health, and linguistics, there is likely to be a strong rebirth of interest in classical conditioning in the next decade.

Razran's reports (1960, 1961) on *interoceptive conditioning* imply an extension of the conditioning paradigm to problems of a *psychosomatic* nature. Further, the theoretical implications of the work on interoceptive conditioning seem to question the Freudian interpretations of psychosomatic phenomena in terms of an *inferred unconscious*.

Interoceptors refer to sensory receptors in the internal organs or viscera in body cavities, e.g., in the stomach, intestines, and heart. "Interoceptive conditioning," therefore, refers to conditioned responses in which one or both of the stimuli (the CS and the US) are applied to one of the viscera rather than to an *exteroceptor,* i.e., an external receptor.

Razran (1960, 1961) reports that Soviet physiologists have completed approximately a hundred studies in which at least one stimulus was applied to one of the viscera. The work is discussed within the context of the *observable unconscious,* a term used to refer to controlled formation of habits with no awareness, motivation, or particular effort on the part of the subject.

As an illustration of one type of interoceptive conditioning, let us assume that we have six healthy human subjects who have volunteered to swallow inflatable tubes which will permit the experimenter to provide selected stimuli directly to the stomach cavity, or if inflated with air and attached to a plethysmograph (a device for measuring size of a limb or organ), will permit observation of stomach contractions. If warm water is injected into the tube a plethysmographic record will indicate vasodilation, whereas if cold water is used, the record will show vasoconstriction.

Since these thermal stimuli produce a highly predictable vascular response, they may be used as unconditioned stimuli. Following the classical conditioning paradigm, it now is necessary only to present a CS, a stimulus which does not elicit a vascular response, in close contiguity with a thermal stimulus to the stomach cavity, to produce a conditioned vascular response. Thus, if we use as a CS the verbal command "blush" and as a US 100 milliliters of water at 43°C injected into the inflatable tubes that our six subjects have swallowed, we would obtain a CR of vasodilation to develop to the command "blush." Soviet investigators have reported several successful studies in which the UR was vascular, the US was presented via an inflatable tube to the viscera, and the CS was external.

In several studies, the CS has been applied directly to the viscera, frequently through a fistula (opening) to a body cavity. Indirect stimulation of the viscera may serve as a US also. When electric shock is applied to the leg of an organism, flexion of the leg occurs. Many other responses, including cardiac acceleration, also occur. Electric shock, therefore, can be used as a US for cardiac acceleration. If a light tactual stimulus is applied to the stomach it will be found to have little effect on cardiac response; however, if a tactual stimulus to the stomach (CS) is paired with electric shock to the leg (US), a conditioned response will develop in which a tactual stimulus to the stomach, such as food or contraction of an empty stomach, will elicit cardiac acceleration.

The implications for theories of psychosomatic disorders of conditioning the internal organs to internal and external stimuli are great indeed. One result of this work may be the development of therapeutic techniques for reconditioning viscera for which a maladaptive habit has been formed. There are significant implications, too, for those theories of personality and motivation in which the Freudian conceptualization of the unconscious plays a central role.

interoceptors	Interoceptors refer to sensory receptors in the internal organs or viscera in the body cavities. The sensory receptors of the stomach are an example of _____.
external	If interoceptors refer to sensory receptors in the *internal* organs, then exteroceptors refer to _____ sensory receptors.
interoceptive internal organs interoceptors	Interoceptive conditioning refers to conditioned responses in which one or both of the stimuli (the CS and the US) are applied to the viscera. If a tactual stimulus is applied to a portion of the intestines (CS), followed by an electric shock (US) to a limb, an increase in the acceleration of the heart (CR) will be noted. Thus, when food products pass through that portion of the intestine, the CR occurs. This is an example of _____ conditioning, for the CS was applied to sensory receptors in the _____, called _____.

When the thermal stimulus to the stomach was paired with the verbal command "blush," the US was applied _____ while the _____ was applied externally.

internally
CS

It is apparent, then, that for interoceptive conditioning to occur, _____ or both stimuli must be applied internally.

one

It becomes apparent through interoceptive conditioning that habit formation may occur (with, without) awareness or motivation on the part of the subject.

without

The term "observable unconscious" has been used to refer to the formation of habits with no awareness or specific effort on the part of the subject. The acceleration of the heart as a result of food passing a point in the intestines would be an example of the _____ because the subject had (awareness, no awareness) of the basis for the increase in heart rate.

observable
unconscious
no awareness

One of the distinguishing characteristics which separate interoceptive conditioning and Freudian psychology is the fact that Freudian psychologists cannot _____ a psychosomatic phenomenon directly.

observe

○ If the conditions listed below are such that interoceptive conditioning could occur, write "yes"; otherwise, write "no."

_____1. CS and US both presented internally

yes

_____2. CS presented internally, US presented externally

yes

_____3. CS presented externally, US presented internally

yes

_____4. CS presented externally, US presented externally

no

THEORETICAL CONSIDERATIONS

As one of the eminent scientists of this century, Pavlov was aware of the importance of theory as a means of generating new hypotheses. Since he was a physiologist, his theory of conditioning (1927) was conceptualized in cortical terms. In his artificial model, a two-dimensional brain is postulated, as are two major functions of the cortex, *excitation* and *inhibition*. Pavlov proposed that a positive US, for example, food, generated excitation at a specific point on the cortex and that the excitation spread or irradiated to surrounding areas of the cortex. A negative US, for example, shock, generates inhibition at a specific point and irradiates to surrounding areas. Stimuli other than the US also generate excitations or inhibitions which irradiate from their specific points to other areas of the cortex. During the acquisition phase of conditioning, therefore, the CS generates excitation at one point on the cortex and the US at another point. The excitation spreads over part of the cortex from each point, and the amount of the spread is, in part, a function of the intensity of stimulation. It is hypothesized further that the *weaker* excitation aroused by the CS is drawn to and concentrated in the *stronger* excitation generated by the US. Pavlov said, "Under suitable conditions a new connection must be formed at the very first occurrence of the stimulus excitation and become strengthened by every repetition." In effect, Pavlov hypothesized that a habit is established upon the first cortical association of a CS and a US, and that *the function of practice,* i.e., of further pairings, *is to increase habit strength,* a notion which has played an important role in several American theories of learning.

Since the CS is a member of a class of stimuli, presentation of a related stimulus (stimulus generalization) results in excitation which is readily drawn to the excitation center of the US or to the center for CS_1. However, if CS_2 is not reinforced but CS_1 is always reinforced (discrimination), CS_2 ceases to generate excitation and becomes inhibitory.

Pavlov believed that conditioning always occurred against an "inhibitory background." During the acquisition of a CR, neutral stimuli present in the situation are inhibitory; hence, they depress the CR and can be considered to be *conditioned inhibitors.* If the CS is followed for several trials by a neutral stimulus, a supernormal response occurs when the CS is presented again, a process which Pavlov called *positive induction.* In this process, presentation of the neutral stimulus for several trials produces inhibition which irradiates over the cortex. When the CS is presented again, its excitation is intensified. One may look upon this phenomenon as a case of *perceptual contrast. Negative induction,* another case of perceptual contrast, results in a subnormal response, for in this case inhibition effects are intensified through the addition of an excitatory stimulus.

Pavlovian theory of inhibitory processes in conditioning was developed from studies of appetitive behavior but it has been found to be applicable to aversive behavior, for example, pain and fear. Thus, an experimenter can reduce pain and fear in the aversive conditioning of an experimental subject by adding a conditioned inhibitor occasionally.

Of what value is the Pavlovian theory of cortical function during learning? Certainly, one cannot accept literally the concept of a two-dimensional brain, nor can one accept uncritically the doubtful physiological processes hypothesized. To be useful, a theory must be able to handle significant data from a range of studies, and if this criterion for the validity of a theory is accepted, Pavlov's theorizing does account rather well for the acquisition and the extinction of CSs under both appetitive and aversive stimulation.

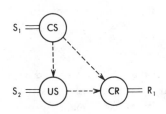

Fig. 2 Stimulus substitution. The stimulus S_1 is ineffective with respect to eliciting the response R prior to learning. S_2 is the adequate stimulus. Broken arrows indicate the associational routes whereby S_1 might become the sufficient stimulus. The direct CS-CR route has the advantage of theoretical simplicity. Where evidence points to a CS-US route, the problem becomes a neurophysiological one but has behavioral implications. This implies, for example, that the response may be blocked temporarily during learning without disruption of the acquisition process. Some instances of stimulus substitution require this S-S explanation. [R. H. Waters, D. A. Rethlingshafer, and W. E. Caldwell (Eds.). **Principles of comparative psychology.** New York: McGraw-Hill, 1960, p. 188.]

On a more general level, classical conditioning has been related to *contiguity theories of learning,* in which primary emphasis is placed on the close, contiguous *association* of two or more stimuli (CS-US) or of a stimulus and a response rather than on the *effect* of a response on the environment. In Pavlovian conditioning the spatial-temporal contiguity of the CS and the US has been shown to be critical to learning. It is important to note, however, that Pavlov assigned reinforcement properties, in an empirical sense, to the US. Conditioning does not occur simply from the *frequency* of paired presentations of any two stimuli; one stimulus must be capable of eliciting a response. Because of this, conditioning has been interpreted as a *stimulus substitution.* (See Fig. 2.) The CS is said to become a substitute for the US, although it is clear that the CS cannot be more than a partial substitute, a signal for the coming of the US. If the emphasis is placed on the *signalizing* function of the CS, an interpretation of conditioning in terms of *expectancy theory* is possible. The presentation of the CS tells or signals the organism to anticipate or expect the US to follow. The expectancy interpretation of conditioning appears to be an extension of the meaning of stimulus substitution with a stress on the role of cognition.

excitation

Pavlov believed that the cortex served two major functions, one of which was *excitation.* Consistent with this theory, the presentation of food (US) would generate _____ at a point in the cortex.

spread

He believed also that the excitation spread over the cortex and that the amount of spread was related to the intensity of the stimuli. An electric shock of high intensity would produce a greater _____ of excitation than a shock of low intensity.

CS

When a US and a CS are paired in the acquisition phase of conditioning, Pavlov believed that the weaker stimulus, the _____ was drawn to or concentrated in the greater excitation generated by the US.

Thus, the US-_____ connection is   CS
formed at the very first occurrence, when the CS
is drawn to the _____ excitation.   greater

Since all positive stimuli, whether USs or CSs,
produce some cortical excitation, one might expect a CS to produce (more, less) excitation   less
than a US.

In Pavlov's classical experiment using meat powder and a bell as stimuli, the spread of excitation resulting from the US, the _____,   meat powder
would be (greater, less) than the spread of   greater
_____ of the CS, the bell, and thus   excitation
the excitation would be drawn to the stronger
stimulus.

If the US-CS connection is formed on the first
cortical _____, the further pairings   association
serve to increase habit strength.

According to this theory, if Pavlov's dog had
not made a _____ in the first trial,   cortical
further practice would have been of no   association
value. Thus, additional trials merely increase
_____ and are not related to the   habit strength
organism's ability to make the initial association
between US and CS.

Since CS_1 is a member of a class of stimuli, CS_2
is also drawn to the center of _____.   excitation

Recalling the unit on discrimination, if CS_2 is
not reinforced but CS_1 is, you would expect CS_2
to (generate, cease to generate) excitation.   cease to generate

Thus, for the animal that is taught to discriminate between a yellow (CS_1) and a blue (CS_2)
light, CS_2 ceases to generate _____   excitation

60

at a point in the cortex and thus becomes inhibitory.

○ As was stated earlier, Pavlov believed that the cortex served two major functions: _____ and inhibition.

excitation

During the acquisition of a CR, neutral stimuli present in the situation are inhibitory, depressing the CR; thus, they are considered to be conditioned inhibitors. If a bell is sounded while an animal is being conditioned to a CS of light, the _____ would function as a conditioned inhibitor.

bell

The effects of a neutral stimulus can be overcome by *following* the CS on several trials with a neutral stimulus. When the CS is presented again, a *supernormal* response occurs. If the US is meat powder, the CS is a light, the CR is salivation, and the neutral stimulus is a bell, what should be the effect on salivation if presentation of the CS is followed by several presentations of the bell? _____

increase in
salivation

The presentation of a _____ stimulus for several trials produces inhibition which irradiates over the cortex.

neutral

○ *Positive induction*, the process of presenting the neutral stimulus following the CS for several trials, results in a _____ response to the CS.

supernormal

According to Pavlov, the supernormal response to the CS is the result of *perceptual contrast*. Specifically, the CS excites the cortex while the several presentations of the neutral stimulus

_____ this stimulus, allowing a greater spread of excitation from the _____ stimulus.

inhibit

conditioned

○ A supernormal response to a CS which has been followed for several trials by a neutral stimulus is called _____, and according to Pavlovian theory, it is a result of _____.

positive induction

perceptual contrast

○ Just as positive induction results in a supernormal response, one would expect _____ induction to result in a subnormal response.

negative

○ Complete the following statements, making them consistent with Pavlov's theory of conditioning:
  1. The spread of excitation is directly related to the _____.
  2. The presence of a neutral stimulus (increases, decreases) excitation.
  3. The process of presenting several trials of a neutral stimulus which increases the level of responding is called _____.
  4. Pavlov argues that supernormal responses are a result of perceptual contrast. What does he mean by "perceptual contrast"?

_____

_____

strength of the stimulus

decreases

positive induction

The repeated presentation of the neutral stimulus causes it to be inhibitory, thus allowing the greater spread of the excitation from the CS.

62

It can be seen that classical conditioning is based on the close contiguous association of two

stimuli

or more _____ rather than on the effects of a response on the environment.

classical

For this reason, _____ conditioning has been related to contiguity theories of learning.

A light elicits a response after being paired with an electric shock. This habit could be inter-

contiguity

preted within a _____ theory of learning.

CS

Because the _____ (stimulus) tends to serve as a substitute for the US in eliciting a response, conditioning is often referred to as

substitution

stimulus _____.

It has also been argued that the emphasis should be placed on the signaling function of the CS. Thus, the CS leads the organism to *expect* the onset of the US. For these theorists, conditioning

expectancy

is explained in terms of _____ theory rather than as stimulus substitution.

○ According to Pavlovian theory, the effects of

excitatory
inhibitory

stimuli on the cortex are either _____ or _____.

○ Classical conditioning is often classified as

contiguity

a _____ theory of learning.

○ The function of the CS relative to the US usually has been explained in two ways:

stimulus
  substitution
expectancy
  theory

1. _____

2. _____

CONCLUDING COMMENTS ON CLASSICAL CONDITIONING

In classical conditioning we have examined a rather elementary form of learning consisting of the simple association of two classes of stimuli, one of which must be reinforcing in the sense that it will elicit a response upon each presentation and one of which fails initially to elicit the response in question. Conditioned-response learning occurs in the simplest organisms, such as the planarian, as well as in complex organisms, such as man. It is important to note that it is a form of learning that does not require a motivated organism, in the sense of an organism whose behavior is goal directed. In fact, CRs have been established in animals in which much of the brain has been removed.

In the classical conditioning paradigm, the emphasis is placed on *association* between the CS and the US, that is to say, on the temporal arrangements between the stimuli. In operant learning, in contrast, the emphasis is placed on the consequences of the subject's responses to the environment and the reinforcement of those responses. Further, in the classical conditioning procedures, the experimenter controls the CS and the US precisely, and thus he controls the response under observation. The organism should not be considered to be passive; yet it is clear that it has no control over the situation, that is, the environment is not brought under the organism's control by the effects of its responses. *The CS-US presentation is fixed and invariable. Hence, the organism's responses do not terminate the US; the experimenter terminates it.* As the reader will discover in the next unit, the procedures used in the study of operants differ primarily on the points discussed in this paragraph.

It is probably erroneous to dismiss the conditioning paradigm as unimportant to learning in the higher organisms. A wide range of stimuli can be made to elicit many classes of responses, although these responses typically are considered "involuntary," a term which implies that the responses are of little consequence in the types of things humans learn. The fact that conditioned responses are reflexive, largely autonomic, and do not require an organism to work actively toward a goal should not be construed to mean that the habits acquired play a minor role in the organism's interactions and transactions with his environment. The studies of interoceptive conditioning indicate that the internal environment, specifically that in which a host of emotional responses occur, deserves intensive investigation within the rubric of the conditioning model.

Perhaps of equal significance with the work on interoceptive conditioning are the American and Russian studies of *semantic conditioning,* which Razran has defined as ". . . the conditioning of a reflex to a word or sentence irrespective of the particular constituent letters or sounds of the word or the particular constituent words of the sentence: that is, conditioning to meaning" (1961, p. 99). In these studies, words (CSs) in a meaningful verbal context have been conditioned to a variety of responses such as salivation, vasoconstriction, blood coagulation, vasodilation, and limb flexion. The discovery of direct links between visceral reactions, such as cardiac rate, vasodilation, and vasoconstriction, and verbal symbols (including their meanings) has fascinating implications for the treatment of psychosomatic disorders. The extension of the classical conditioning paradigm to cognitive processes also promises to lead to research of significance to language development and thinking. In recent years, classical conditioning techniques have been extended to an analysis of the process of perception (Sokolov, 1963) and to the treatment of behavior disorders (Ban, 1964; Group for the Advancement of Psychiatry, 1964; Lovibond, 1964; Wolpe, Salter, and Reyna, 1964; Grossberg, 1964). The range of problems treated with some success includes enuresis, tics, fetishes, phobias, writer's cramp, alcoholism, stuttering, and anxiety reactions. For example, in the treatment of alcoholism, a conditioned aversion may be developed by administering a nausea-inducing drug (US) in association with alcohol (CS). Other unconditioned stimuli, for example, electroshock, have been used with some success in the treatment of alcoholism.

The use of conditioning techniques in the treatment of bedwetting has been supported by recent research (Lovibond, 1964). The original method of treatment (Mowrer, 1938) consisted of a bell and a pad wired in a circuit so that when the child wet the pad slightly, the circuit was completed, the bell rang, awakening the child well before the bladder was emptied. Bladder distention is the CS which is paired with the bell (US), a cue for awakening. In several studies, the habit was extinguished in a large proportion of the patients with no increase in anxiety or substitution of other symptoms.

Finally, one gets the impression that only one response, the response designated the UR, is conditioned to one stimulus, the CS. As noted earlier, the CS is a member of a class of stimuli many members of which come to elicit the UR (stimulus generalization). In most cases stimuli present in the experimental situation other than the CS may become conditioned also. *Responses other than the UR may become conditioned to the CS during training.* Pavlov called the responses which are preparatory to the UR *orienting reflexes* but he gave them little consideration since he was not directly interested in cognitive processes. Russian investigators have studied these responses in the past decade, representing an additional extension of the classical conditioning paradigm to perceptual-cognitive phenomena. The fact that *more than one response* may be involved in conditioning deserves emphasis since it has become customary for psychologists to refer to "the conditioned response," implying that a UR has become attached to or correlated with a new stimulus, whereas, in fact, the CR may differ from the UR *both* qualitatively and quantitatively. The CR may be weaker than the UR, it may be only a fractional part of the UR, or it may be a different response in its essentials.

Instrumental Learning 3

But it is possible that the most rapid progress toward an
understanding of learning may be made by research
which is not designed to test theories. An
adequate impetus is supplied by the inclination to
obtain data showing orderly characteristics
of the learning process (B. F. Skinner).

INTRODUCTION

In the very short span of time since the publication of *The Behavior of Organisms* in 1939, B. F. Skinner's work has had a substantial effect on psychology. Two of his publications, *Science and Human Behavior* and *Walden Two,* have been read so widely by nonpsychologists that they probably have influenced the views of laymen toward psychology as much as any books published on behavior since World War II. As noted earlier, Skinner distinguished two classes of behavior, *respondent* and *operant,* and he has focused his attention on the latter class. Further, in the tradition of E. L. Thorndike rather than in that of Pavlov, the stress is placed on the effects or *consequences of responding* rather than on *contiguity of stimuli.* What the organism first does *to* the environment takes precedence over what the environment first does *for* the organism. The concern is with responses *emitted* rather than with responses *elicited* and attention is focused on orderly *changes* in behavior rather than on habits as finally established.

From the tradition of trial-and-error learning rather than from conditioned-response learning, Skinner and his associates have de-

(a)

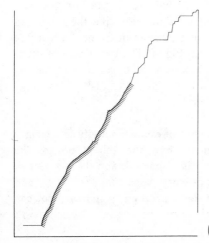

Fig. 3 (a) Rat conditioning apparatus.
(b) A cumulative response record for a rat on a fixed-ratio
extinction schedule of reinforcement. Each slash in the record
represents one bar press.

(b)

68

veloped instrumental-training procedures which enable an investigator to conduct a functional analysis of the behavior of an organism in a *free-response* setting, that is, in a setting in which the organism can move about and act upon the environment. Skinner designed an apparatus, the Skinner box, shown in Fig. 3, consisting of a small chamber with three bare walls and one wall from which a lever or bar projected.

In the typical Skinner box for rats food and water receptacles are located below a lever, and two small lights are above it. Sound is introduced into the box through a speaker. The floor of the chamber is a grid through which electric shock can be applied to the feet of the rats. Food, shock, water, lights, and sound (and, in a sense, the lever) are the stimuli which the experimenter can control in the apparatus as described. All of these can be operated and scheduled automatically by the addition to the chamber of the necessary switching circuits. When a hungry rat is placed in the chamber, exploratory behavior occurs, and sooner or later, the organism presses the bar, an act which has no "meaning" to a naïve subject. When the bar is pressed, a small food pellet is ejected into the feeding chamber and, in time, the rat will discover the pellet and consume it. It probably will resume exploration of the chamber with more attention to the area containing the lever and it soon will learn that bar pressing produces food; thus, the only dependent variable is frequency of bar pressing, or *rate of response*. If a recording device is attached to the apparatus, a record of the frequency of bar pressing per unit of time becomes available for analysis and it might look like the record in Fig. 3. Some representative apparatus for use in instrumental learning with animals and children is shown in Fig. 4. The experimental situation represented by the Skinner box has been generalized across species, from fish to man, and to a large variety of tasks, from lever pressing to verbal behavior.

cannot

response

During the course of random activity of a hungry rat in a Skinner box, the animal presses the lever, a pellet is dispensed, and the rat eats it. One (can, cannot) conclude that the food elicited the lever-pressing response. He can conclude only that the _____ was *emitted*.

(a)   (b)

(c)

Fig. 4 (a) A cumulative response recorder. (Scientific Prototype
Mfg. Corp.)

(b) Monkey working to avoid
punishment in an instrumental
training apparatus which presents
stimuli and records responses
automatically. (Foringer & Co.,
Inc.)

(c) Visual test module. Visual
stimuli are displayed simultaneously in each of the apertures
and the subject presses the sur-
face of the aperture to indicate
his choice of stimulus. (Foringer
& Co., Inc.)

food

If the rat receives a pellet after each *chance* depression of the lever, it learns that pressing the lever produces _____.

emitted

Since no stimulus is used to evoke a response, we can say that the response was _____ rather than elicited.

consequence of
   responding
purposeful

If the rat's trial-and-error pressing of the bar is to become purposeful, it is dependent on the consequences of responding. In this case, food was the _____ and the trial-and-error responding became _____ responding.

rat A
food

Two hungry, untrained rats are placed in identical training boxes. In the course of exploring the apparatus, both rats press the bars in their respective cages. Rat A receives a food pellet each time he presses the bar; rat B receives nothing. Which rat will learn to press the bar when he is hungry? _____ In this example, what is the reinforcer? _____

emitted
reinforcer

It becomes apparent that if learning is to take place in operant (instrumental) training, a response must first be _____, then followed by a _____.

elicited

By contrast, in respondent learning, you will recall that for learning to take place, a stimulus-response connection must exist. In this case, the response is said to be (elicited, emitted).

reinforcing

Thus, operants are under the control of the _____ stimuli which follow them.

instrumental

From the discussion, it is clear that the terms "operant learning" and "_____ learning" are used interchangeably.

In an experiment, rat B is reinforced after every bar press, and rat A is not reinforced. One would expect the *rate* of responding of rat B to _____ and that of rat A to _____.

increase
decrease or
  remain low

To determine whether learning has occurred in instrumental training, one can observe the orderly _____ in responses (rate or frequency of responding) as a function of a _____ stimulus.

change

reinforcing

○ The typical Skinner box used in conditioning has a number of characteristics with which the student should be familiar. A description of a Skinner box is given on page 68. Name five stimuli which an experimenter can manipulate in a Skinner box:

 1. _____
 2. _____
 3. _____
 4. _____
 5. _____

food
light
water
shock
sound

A cumulative recording device is pictured on page 69. Its purposes are two: (1) to record _____ per unit of time and (2) to record the number of reinforcements per unit of time.

responses

Under continuous reinforcement, one bar press will produce _____ pellet, which serves to _____ the response.

one
reinforce

You will recall that extinction of a response in respondent conditioning is obtained by terminating the _____ while continuing to

US

CS present the _____. A response learned under operant conditioning would be extin-
reinforcement guished by terminating the _____ of the response.

○ Listed below are the characteristics that distinguish operant learning from respondent learning. Label each one appropriately:

operant _____1. Emitted responses
respondent _____2. Elicited responses
respondent _____3. Unlearned S-R connection
respondent _____4. The contiguity of stimuli
operant _____5. Consequences of responding
operant _____6. A response produces a re-inforcer
operant _____7. Instrumental training
operant _____8. The termination of reinforcement produces extinction
operant _____9. Exploratory behavior is important

THREE EXAMPLES OF OPERANT LEARNING

Before proceeding with a discussion of the structure, concepts, and procedures of instrumental training, three examples of operant learning are presented to provide the reader with descriptions of the full process of shaping behavior. The examples should be kept in mind while reading about the separate parts; otherwise, one will have difficulty in integrating and synthesizing the components of the formal procedures used in instrumental training. In Exhibit 4 a familiar organism is taught an unusual task. Since many readers will have had experience in informal training of a pet, the procedures described will be easy to grasp. The formal training of a child as an object of scientific investigation is described in Exhibit 5. The systematic manipulation of one or more independent variables for the purpose of observing their effects on the behavior of a child promises to provide empirical support for scientific child psychology. The third example of instrumental training, presented in Exhibit 6 involves a preliminary investigation of the effectiveness of the technique in teaching severely handicapped children to read.

EXHIBIT 4

INFORMAL TRAINING OF A DOG

In an article entitled "How to Teach Animals," B. F. Skinner describes a number of habits which can be taught to animals outside the laboratory. An example of a habit of this type would be teaching a pet dog to answer questions by having it point its head to "yes" or "no" as appropriate. It is only necessary to have it learn to distinguish two cues from its master, one for "no" and one for "yes," and to respond to the cues differentially. At the beginning of the training, it is assumed that the dog already responds well to a number of commands—that it is a rather obedient subject.

The first step is to link approach to two signs containing the word "no" and the word "yes," with food reinforcement. When this operant occurs reliably, that is, when the dog approaches the signs to be fed on the command "here," the next step can be undertaken. Instead of feeding the dog for approach to the signs on command, the master next feeds (i.e., reinforces) only when the dog approaches the sign on which the master places his hand; thus the animal must learn to attend to the master's hand. When this has been accomplished, another discrimination will be required, a discrimination between one finger over the top of a card and four fingers over the top of a card. One finger is the cue for pointing the head toward "yes," and four fingers is the cue for pointing the head toward "no." Once these responses have been learned—and an obedient dog can learn them—the master is ready to demonstrate his dog's ability to answer any question which can be satisfactorily answered with a "yes" or "no."

Animal trainers have successfully trained several species, including dogs, to respond differentially to much more subtle clues, e.g., slight movements of facial muscles as a cue for counting or solving a series of problems such as the square root of 4, 9, 16, and 25.

EXHIBIT 5

FORMAL TRAINING OF A CHILD

In a series of articles S. W. Bijou (e.g., 1957, 1958) and his colleagues described several successful applications of instrumental training to young children that enabled them to undertake systematic studies of functional relationships in children's behavior.

One instrumental-training laboratory described by Bijou is a room equipped with a one-way mirror and containing two tables, one holding a display case with two toys in it and the other holding two pieces of apparatus, one to dispense candy and one containing a panel with two lights and a handle.

In this appealing setting, the child is encouraged to play with the toys and to manipulate the handle as he desires. He is told when he enters the laboratory that he will be able to take home any trinkets he is given. Naturally, many children explore the room, play with the toys, and usually, manipulate the handle within a few minutes after entering the room. The child's behavior is monitored by the investigator through the one-way-vision mirror. Once the child discovers the *contingency* (relationship) between lever or handle pressing and receipt of a trinket, a piece of candy, or a token, it is possible to determine his rate of response to the mechanism. Then one can introduce an independent variable and determine its effects on his rate of responding. A cumulative recorder is used to obtain a record of responses and reinforcement.

Through this technique, it is possible to investigate many of the same variables of learning in children as have been investigated in laboratory animals and to compare and contrast the parameters of these variables across species. This enables psychologists to determine the validity of their extrapolations from findings on animals to humans. In addition, a functional analysis of the behaviors of children is of significance in its own right.

EXHIBIT 6*

The purpose of this report is to describe the development and utility of a technique developed specifically to train congenital deaf-mutes with diagnosed mental retardation to read. The technique to be described is a modification of the "oddity problem"—a problem in discriminative learning which has been applied to various animals, including the rat (Wodinsky and Bitterman, 1953), cat (Boyd and Warren, 1957; Warren, 1960) and monkey (Moon and Harlow, 1955).

GENERAL PROCEDURE

Method

The oddity problem consists of presenting the subject with several stimuli all but one of which are identical. The S's task is to respond to the stimuli by indicating the odd stimulus of the sample. When correct discrimination is made S is reinforced in a manner suitable to the species. For example, if the stimuli are X O X, S would select O. Similarly, if O O X were presented, the proper response would be X.

In working with retarded human Ss, four distinct phases of training were used. In Phase I three wood blocks, 4 x 4 x 4 in., were presented to S. The blocks were painted with a different solid color; e.g., red, blue and yellow. Each trial consisted of presenting S with three blocks, two of which were identical in color. The S was taught to select one of the blocks by pushing it from the other. If the odd colored block was selected, S was given a small candy (M & M). A correction procedure was used so that if one of the identical blocks was selected, S was allowed to make another selection until the correct block was chosen. After each correct choice and reinforcement a new trial was begun.

* Candland, D. K., and Conklyn, D. H. Use of the "oddity problem" in teaching mentally retarded deaf-mutes to read; a pilot project. *Train. Sch. Bull.,* 1962, **59,** 38–41. Reprinted with the permission of the authors and the publisher. This study was supported by a grant from the National Institutes of Health, Public Health Service [M = 5698 (A)] to the first author.

In Phase II letters were substituted for the colors on the blocks. The color of the blocks was red and the letters were white and 3 in. high. The procedure of discriminating the odd block (letter) was used. The position of the blocks and the combinations of letters were altered randomly on each trial in order to avoid S's responding to the position of the block rather than to the letter.

When letters were discriminated successfully with consistently greater than chance accuracy, S was required to discriminate words by the same technique. In this phase (III), if the S had learned to discriminate the letters "B", "C", "A" and "T", three 5 x 8 in., cards containing the words "CAT", "BAT", and "BAT" were shown. Again, the task of the S was to select the odd card, in this case "CAT". Note that the three stimuli differ only in one letter—B or C.

The final phase of training (IV) consisted of presenting S with pictures of objects which corresponded to the words that had been discriminated successfully. In this phase, S was required to match the picture with the word. In addition to the common nouns which were taught by picture, simple action verbs were taught by the E's performing the action. In this manner such verbs as "run" and "sit" were matched with nouns by the S into simple sentences.

Subjects

A test was given to potential Ss in order to determine whether each had previous verbal or written experience with the words used in the experiment. A series of pictures; e.g., cat and dog, was given to the Ss. If S showed any indication of either verbal or written knowledge of the object the word was not used in the experiment.

The procedure reported here was evolved on four Ss. All Ss were congenital deaf-mutes; all were considered verbally un-educable; all were rated with IQ's between 41 and 60 (Leiter International Performance Scale). Since these Ss served primarily to allow refinement of the phases of the procedure, the results of the complete technique as applied to the fourth S will be described. This S was 12-years old at the onset of experimentation. The institutional diagnosis of this S was congenital deafness from natal brain damage; MA 5 years, 2 months. The S had been a resident of the institution for four years. From information available, S had never received any form of verbal training and was considered to be uneducable.

Results

Phase I (oddity training)   The S was able to discriminate the odd color from the sample with 70% accuracy (chance = 33%) after five, 30-minute sessions of 30 trials each. A negatively accelerated learning curve resulted with S performing at chance accuracy during the first session and improving to the 70% level by the third session. This plateau in performance was retained through the fifth session. Although it is likely that some Ss would reach a higher performance level, the S used in this study did not pass the 70% level of accuracy within the number of sessions allowed for this phase.

Phase II (transfer to letters)   In this phase, 14 different letters were presented to S. They were A, B, C, D, G, I, L, M, N, O, R, S, T and U. After nine 30-minute sessions of 30 trials each, the S was able to discriminate the letters from one another with 68% accuracy. (chance = 33%).

Phase III (word discrimination)   The S was able to discriminate seven words within 12, 30-minute sessions. These nouns were cat, dog, man, girl, ball, and the verbs were sit and run. The criterion of discrimination was successful discrimination on at least 90% of the presentations.

Phase IV (association with pictures)   In the final stage of training S was able to associate all five nouns with the appropriate pictures and both verbs with the appropriate motions. This was accomplished in 13 sessions of 30-minutes each.

Discussion

The significance of the results of this pilot work is in the indication that the technique of the oddity-problem, adapted from research with animals, may be useful in teaching congenital deaf-mutes with presumed mental retardation to read. It is possible, of course, that the technique can be extended in some cases to teaching Ss to write by substituting the response of writing for that of choosing manually, as was done in this work. Similarly, this technique might be useful for Ss who are neither deaf-mute nor mentally retarded.

The technique described here can be instrumented easily in order to allow S continuous access to the stimuli. In this manner, S can work at the task when his motivation is high and several Ss may use the same machine, thus eliminating the cost in time and money of a trained operator. In this respect, the technique has the same technical advantages as many teaching-machines which may be adapted for use with deaf or retarded children (Porter, 1957). Indeed, several problem-solving apparatus are currently marketed which are modified easily to present the oddity problem.

Several research questions suggest themselves regarding refinements in technique. Throughout the experiment a ratio of two similar stimuli to one dissimilar stimulus was used. This 2:1 ratio is, of course, the lowest possible ratio for the oddity problem. On the other hand, it is possible that a larger ratio (e.g., 4:1 or 5:1) would lead to more rapid learning.

Finally, in the studies reported here continuous reinforcement (FR 1:1) was used. Although this type of reinforcement leads to rapid learning, it does not necessarily lead to strongest retention if extinction is taken as the criterion of retention. (Ferster and Skinner, 1957). It is possible that retention of the discriminations would be greater if a variable ratio schedule of reinforcement was employed when the response had become stable (e.g., Phase III).

Summary

A technique is reported for teaching congenital deaf-mutes with reported mental retardation to read. The technique is based on the "oddity-problem"—a problem of discriminative behavior used in animal research. The findings indicate that the technique may be applied successfully. Research problems concerned with refinement of the technique are discussed.*

* References for this article appear on p. 120.

REINFORCEMENT

One of the critical distinctions between classical conditioning and instrumental learning lies in the meaning of the term "reinforcement." For Pavlov, the US was said to be a reinforcer, and any event which strengthened behavior was called "reinforcement"; however, since the US was always paired with another stimulus, the CS, it follows that the strengthening must be of an *association between stimuli*. In instrumental learning or operant training, *the reinforcing stimulus is produced by, or is the consequence of, a response;* therefore, the association which is strengthened is that of a response and its consequence, providing that the consequence increases the probability, or the frequency with which the response occurs. Clearly, the experimenter's procedures in relationship to stimulus-and-response events in classical conditioning and in instrumental learning are quite different. The exact nature of a "consequence," or a reinforcement, is still to be determined. Although, in conventional usage, writers refer to a reinforcing event and a reinforcing stimulus as if they were synonomous, research on this problem seems to indicate that a reinforcing event may have at least three meanings: (1) the presentation or termination of a stimulus, (2) a change in stimulation, and (3) the opportunity to emit a response of high probability (Hundt and Premack, 1963; Homme and Tosti, 1965). In this text, "reinforcer" is used to mean an event, without specifying in each instance whether the event is thought to be a stimulus only, a response only, or both. Knowing something about the motivational state of the organism and providing a goal or incentive which will interact with the motivational state is prerequisite to operant training. In fact, *the motivational state of the subject is so important that it affects rate of extinction as well as rate of acquisition of a habit.* As a general rule, it is found in rats that rate of extinction can be lengthened by a factor of two or three simply by increasing the level of food deprivation. It would seem that when reinforcement involves the presentation of an incentive which interacts with an existing motivational state, the meaning of reinforcement differs sharply from Pavlov's use of the term as equivalent to any US.

In Pavlovian conditioning the reinforcer is said to be the _____ stimulus.   unconditioned

In classical conditioning the US always is paired

80

Answers	
CS	with the _____, and thus learning is thought to result from an association between _____.
stimuli	
operant	In instrumental or _____ learning, the reinforcing event (S^r) is produced by or is a consequence of a _____ rather than a stimulus.
response	
stimuli	Thus, in respondent learning we are concerned with the association of two _____, while in instrumental learning we are concerned with the association of a _____ and its _____.
response	
consequence	
hunger	For the consequence of the response in instrumental learning to be reinforcing, it must interact with the motivational state of the organism. Food will not be reinforcing to a dog unless he is motivated by a _____ drive.
motivational	Another factor which distinguishes operant learning from classical conditioning is the _____ state of the organism.
less rapidly	The motivational state of the organism affects extinction as well as acquisition. One would expect a dog which has been deprived of food for four days to extinguish (more rapidly, less rapidly) than a dog deprived of food for twelve hours.
classical conditioning	○ Place either "classical conditioning" or "instrumental learning" before each of the following:
	_____1. The US is the reinforcing agent.
instrumental learning	_____2. The reinforcer is a consequence of the response.

            3. There is an association be-   instrumental
                 tween the response and its   learning
                 consequence.
            4. Information concerning the   instrumental
                 motivational state of the or-   learning
                 ganism is an important con-
                 dition for training.
            5. Learning is the result of a   classical
                 pairing of stimuli.   conditioning

Primary and secondary reinforcement

Typically, in laboratory studies of operant conditioning, incentives such as food, water, and electric shock, are used which interact directly with the motivational state. However, in addition to the use of these primary reinforcers, experimenters have shown great interest in the study of *secondary* or *conditioned reinforcers,* that is, in stimuli which have acquired reinforcing properties. *Stimuli regularly associated with primary reinforcement may themselves acquire the power to strengthen behavior.* Such stimuli as food dishes, water receptacles, sound, light, and color of apparatus are examples of stimuli which come to have secondary reinforcing value in laboratory studies; in other words, they become conditioned reinforcers. Outside the laboratory, almost any stimulus may become a conditioned reinforcer for animal or human behavior according to the arguments of some psychologists.

Whether a stimulus has *incentive value* must be determined empirically. Much of the current controversy over the concept of secondary reinforcement has arisen from attempts to compare studies in which different criteria for the establishment of secondary reinforcement are used. According to one group of experimenters, the issue may be resolved by asking the proper questions, viz., Can the animal learn a *new* response under a *new* motivational state when the reinforcer is the conditioned reinforcer in question? If we have conditioned a group of dogs to escape from an apparatus in which a light always signaled the onset of electric shock, light can be considered a secondary reinforcer if it can be demonstrated that the dogs can acquire a new habit with light as the reinforcer.

For another group of experimenters, a less stringent criterion is used, viz., Does it take longer to extinguish a response, is *resistance to extinction greater,* when the secondary reinforcing stimulus is present than when it is absent? For example, let us assume that pigeons have learned to peck a key for a reward of food in a situation in which a clicking sound always occurs when the key is pecked, and therefore a click always precedes the receipt of the reward. If we then divide our group into two subgroups and extinguish one group in the apparatus in which the pecking of the key produces a click and the other group in an identical apparatus in which the pecking of the key does not produce the click, will the groups differ in the time which is required to extinguish the habit of key pecking? The general finding has been that resistance to extinction is greater when the conditioned reinforcer is present during extinction trials.

If one looks at the magnitude of the effects that supposedly result from the reinforcing properties of previously neutral stimuli, he will find them to be small. If one takes a response, the *operant level* (rate of occurrence) of which may be 10 responses per hour, and uses a conditioned reinforcer to strengthen that response, it is likely that the rate of response will increase rather little, say to 12 responses per hour; yet, the investigator knows that if he provided his subject with something which it needed, such as food or water, the operant level might be increased to 400 responses per hour.

The student must not conclude that such previously neutral stimuli have no motivating properties; in fact, they may have a great deal. The unresolved issue is, Can one convert a previously neutral stimulus into a true reinforcer by using the stimulus in an instrumental-training situation?

EXHIBIT 7

SECONDARY REINFORCEMENT: A TOKEN-REWARD STUDY

The pioneer study on the use of a token or symbolic reinforcer with animals was reported by J. B. Wolfe in 1936. Chimpanzees were taught to obtain food by inserting poker chips into a machine which Wolfe constructed. The chimpanzees quickly learned to associate the chips with the receipt of food. One question which was investigated by Wolfe was whether the chimpanzees would work at a task for a poker chip as the reward for their effort. The task was to lift a weighted handle; when the subject lifted the handle, it received a chip on some of the trials and a grape on the others. The chips, of course, would be inserted into the machine for food. Wolfe found that his animals would work for a token, the poker chip, and that they could delay reinforcement if they were permitted to hold the chips they had earned in their hands. Other investigators (for example, Cowles, 1937) extended Wolfe's work on chimpanzees and found that they could solve new problems when the only reinforcement was a token.

Generalized reinforcers

When a conditioned reinforcer is associated with several primary reinforcers, its reinforcing properties may be *generalized* to a variety of behaviors irrespective of the current motivational state of the organism. Presumably, a great many objects and events in our environment come to be *generalized reinforcers,* such as words, money, food, parents, clothing, cigarettes, alcohol, automobiles, and even the techniques and methods which we use to control our environment successfully. Skinner (1953) has described several generalized reinforcers which are acquired through social reinforcement of our behavior, including such important behavioral processes as attention, approval, affection, and submissiveness.

The concept of secondary or conditioned reinforcers is a necessary supplement to that of primary reinforcers. Since it is clear that a considerable amount of learning occurs during the absence of any relevant primary reinforcement, both in and outside the laboratory, any reinforcement learning theory must provide an explanation of how the learning occurs in the absence of a primary reinforcer. The concept of "conditioned reinforcers" serves that purpose rather nicely.

Stimuli which are regularly associated with primary reinforcement and which acquire the power to strengthen behavior are called "secondary reinforcers." Food for a hungry dog would be considered a _____ reinforcer, while the food dish might become a _____ reinforcer.

primary

secondary

For a food dish to be called a "secondary re-inforcer," it must serve as a substitute for the _____ reinforcer.

primary

If a light flashes each time a hungry dog is given food for pressing a pedal, the light may be considered a secondary reinforcer only if it _____ or maintains the behavior in the absence of food reinforcement.

strengthens

In determining whether the light has reinforcing properties, one would expect the presence of the light during extinction trials to (increase, decrease) resistance to extinction.

increase

If a conditioned or secondary reinforcer—in this case, a light—is associated with several primary reinforcers, food, water, stroking, etc., one would expect the _____ characteristics of the light to become generalized.

reinforcing

○ Complete the following:

1. The function of a reinforcing event in instrumental conditioning is _____.

to strengthen
the response

2. A stimulus which has acquired reinforcing properties is a _____ reinforcer.

secondary or
conditioned

3. Specify two procedures commonly used to determine whether a stimulus has incentive value.

a. _____

Determining
whether an
animal can learn
a new response
under a new
motivational
state using the
conditioned
reinforcer

b. _____

Determining whether resistance to extinction is greater in the presence of a secondary reinforcer

4. Explain the process through which conditioned reinforcers become generalized reinforcers.

_____

A conditioned reinforcer is associated with several primary reinforcers.

SCHEDULES OF REINFORCEMENT

It has been implied thus far that reinforcement of responses must occur each time the response occurs, which is to say that reinforcement must be *continuous* rather than *partial* or *intermittent*. Indeed, until the advent of the Skinner box, continuous reinforcement—a reward or punishment for each response—was the customary approach in learning studies. In a delightful essay, "A Case History in Scientific Method," in which Skinner describes the development of his method and theory, he states:

One pleasant Saturday afternoon I surveyed my supply of dry pellets and, appealing to certain elemental theorems in arithmetic, deduced that unless I spent the rest of that afternoon and evening at the pill machine, the supply would be exhausted by 10:30 Monday morning.

Since I do not wish to deprecate the hypothetico-deductive method, I am glad to testify here to its usefulness. It led me to apply our second principle of unformalized scientific method and to ask myself why *every* press of the lever had to be reinforced. . . . I decided to reinforce a response only once every minute and to allow all other responses to go unreinforced. There were two results: (1) my supply of pellets lasted almost indefinitely and (2) each rat stabilized at a fairly constant rate of responding. (1959, p. 368)

Thus began the formal study of partial reinforcement: first, periodic or interval reinforcement, and later, ratio reinforcement.

Ratio schedules

In a ratio reinforcement schedule, the organism is reinforced as a function of the *number of responses* emitted. In a *fixed-ratio* (FR) schedule, the reinforcement follows a fixed number of responses, for example, every tenth response, and such a schedule would be symbolized as FR 10. Thus, with an operant training apparatus for teaching a child to learn to discriminate the letters of the alphabet, the investigator might specify one piece of candy following each four correct responses, that is FR 4. This indicates that each child has to press a key under a correct letter four times before the candy is received. *Continuous reinforcement* would be an FR 1 schedule, that is, a schedule in which each correct response was followed by a reinforcement. Continuous nonreinforcement, or extinction, would be a schedule in which no response was followed by a reinforcement.

In a *variable-ratio* (VR) schedule of reinforcement, the reinforcer is systematically related to the number of responses; however, instead of occurring after a fixed number, the reinforcing stimulus occurs after a *variable* number of responses. Thus, one can describe the schedule in terms of the average number of responses which must be emitted per reinforcement. In a VR 10 schedule, the organism would receive a reinforcement for every tenth response, *on the average*. This means that, in practice, the reinforcement might occur following almost any number of unreinforced responses from zero to fifty or more, but it must occur following ten responses on the average.

Interval schedules

One may relate reinforcement to *time* as well as to the number of responses, thus creating *interval* schedules of reinforcement. Again, interval schedules may be *fixed* or *variable*. In a *fixed-interval* (FI) schedule, the reinforcing stimulus occurs after the lapse of an interval of time, such as one, five, or ten seconds, stated as FI 1, FI 5, and FI 10. In a *variable-interval* (VI) schedule, reinforcement occurs, *on the average,* once per unit of time, such as once per second stated as VI 1. Under a VI 5 schedule, the organism might receive a reinforcement or two within seconds, then go unreinforced for twenty seconds or more, but reinforcement must occur once every five seconds *on the average.*

Complex schedules

By combining two or more of the four schedules described above, more complex patterns of reinforcement can be provided for an organism. For example, in a *conjunctive* schedule, reinforcement is provided only after the conditions for two schedules of reinforcement have been met. If the schedule is FI 10 FR 10, the organism will be reinforced only when it completes both schedules in either order. Other schedules have been used which require the organism to alternate between two types of schedules, to complete two schedules in tandem order before receiving a reinforcement, or to work on some variation of these.

Skinner was first to report that constant rates of responding would occur when a *partial* or intermittent schedule of reinforcement was used. For example, a rat which continued to respond when given a pellet of food after every third response rather than after every response would be on a _____ schedule of reinforcement.

partial
(intermittent)

In the example above, the rat is on a fixed-ratio (FR) schedule of one reinforcement to _____ responses.

three

The organism is reinforced as a function of the number of responses emitted in a _____ reinforcement schedule.

ratio

In a fixed-ratio schedule, the reinforcement follows a fixed number of responses. FR 8 means that the organism is reinforced after every _____ response.

eighth

An FR 1 schedule also is an example of a _____ schedule, in which the organism is reinforced after _____ response.

fixed-ratio
every (one)

Thus, continuous reinforcement is an _____ schedule.

FR 1

If an organism is first reinforced after four responses, next after eight responses, and then after twelve responses, the ratio of reinforcement on the average is one reinforcement to

eight

_____ responses.

variable

This is an example of a _____-ratio schedule of reinforcement.

If the conditions of reinforcement are changed to provide a pellet of food only at the end of a two-minute interval, reinforcement would be re-

time

lated to _____ instead of to the number of responses.

Assume that one subject is reinforced after each two minutes of time while a second subject is reinforced after each five minutes of time. In this situation, the schedule of reinforcement dif-

interval

fers as a function of the _____ of time.

From the foregoing, it can be concluded that there are two general types of partial reinforcement: first, ratio schedules of reinforcement, and

interval

second, _____ schedules of reinforcement.

responses

Just as the reinforcement occurs after a fixed number of _____ in an FR schedule,

interval
fixed-interval

you would expect that the reinforcement would occur after a fixed _____ of time in a _____ (FI) schedule.

interval

Just as it is possible to vary ratio schedules of reinforcement, it is possible to vary _____ schedules of reinforcement.

An organism that is reinforced on the average once every five seconds is on a_____- interval schedule of reinforcement. This is a VI _____ schedule because the reinforcement occurs on the _____ of once every five seconds.

variable

5

average

More complex schedules of reinforcement can be provided by combining two or more of the _____ (number of) schedules previously described.

four

○ Label each statement below with the schedule of reinforcement (ratio, FR, VR, interval, FI, VI) to which it is related:

_____1. The frequency of reinforcement is dependent upon time.

interval

_____2. Reinforcement depends upon the *average* number of responses.

VR

_____3. Reinforcement occurs following each response.

FR

_____4. A reinforcement occurs after every twelve seconds.

FI

_____5. A reinforcement occurs on the average after every twelve seconds.

VI

_____6. Reinforcement is a function of the number of responses emitted.

ratio

EFFECTS OF SCHEDULES OF REINFORCEMENT

Under continuous reinforcement (FR 1), the acquisition of a habit will be relatively rapid, and the cumulative record will show a rather smooth curve. Variations in the record occur, often as a function of such factors as age, task to be learned, type and level of deprivation, and momentary physiological state. When intermittent reinforcement is under investigation, the cumulative record may look quite different; that is, the rate of response can vary as a function of the particular schedule of reinforcement which is used.

If one reflected on the differences in rate of responding which would be expected between continuous reinforcement and intermittent reinforcement, he would probably reason that acquisition would be more rapid under the continuous reinforcement (CRF) schedule since each correct response (e.g., each key press to a correct letter of the alphabet or each lever press in a rat box) is reinforced and *no extinction occurs*. Under any intermittent schedule, some of the responses are unreinforced, and each of these constitutes an extinction trial. For example, under FR 2, one-half the responses are unreinforced, and under FR 10, 90 per cent of the responses are unreinforced. As a consequence, one would expect the slopes of cumulative curves to vary as a function of the particular schedule of reinforcement used.

If behavior is reinforced at intervals, that is, by a source *external* to the organism, such as a timer, the rate of response is rather stable relative to the frequency of reinforcement. For a fixed-interval schedule, little responding occurs immediately following the receipt of a reinforcer; as time passes, the rate of responding increases gradually; and as the end of the interval nears, the rate of responding attains a maximum. The cumulative record for an FI schedule, therefore, might look like this:

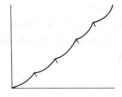

Rate of responding during each interval is steadier for a variable-interval schedule than for an FI schedule since the organism cannot estimate accurately at what point in time the reinforcement will occur. Thus, the cumulative record for a VI schedule might look like this:

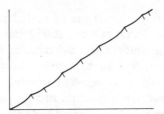

When responses are reinforced as a function of the number of responses emitted, the control is *internal* in that reinforcement is contingent upon the organism's behavior, not on a clock. In a fixed-ratio schedule, the organism is reinforced following a fixed number of responses; as a consequence, a strongly motivated organism will respond rapidly initially, then tend to pause after a reinforcement and increase its rate as it approaches the nth response (the response which is to be reinforced). An FR schedule might look like this:

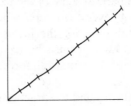

Under a variable-ratio schedule of reinforcement, the rate of reinforcement is dependent upon the rate of response since the organism may be reinforced following a variable number of responses. This schedule tends to produce steady and high rates of responding without the pause associated with a fixed-ratio schedule since the subject cannot predict when a reinforcement might occur. A VR schedule might look like this:

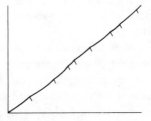

The most interesting phenomena of partial reinforcement are associated with the extinction process. Rapid extinction occurs following training under a continuous reinforcement schedule, while relatively slow extinction, that is, high resistance to extinction, occurs after training on partial reinforcement schedules. Further, resistance to extinction may vary as a function of the type of schedule under which training occurred. Very high resistance to extinction in the form of thousands of unreinforced responses could be obtained under such schedules as FR 500, VI 100, or VR 500. In each of these cases, the organism would become accustomed during acquisition to emitting a large number of responses without receiving reinforcement. In a sense, during extinction under a partial reinforcement schedule, the organism may find it difficult to *discriminate between reinforcement training and extinction*. If the organism "expects" to receive infrequent reinforcement, the difficulty of determining when it is experiencing extinction trials is evident.

Now that we have summarized some of the technical characteristics and some of the effects of several common schedules of intermittent reinforcement, some justification for the inclusion of the topic may be desired by the reader. First, it must be recognized that Skinner's development of the concept of partial reinforcement followed by the invention of several schedules has turned out to be a very significant contribution to both the theory and the practice of psychology. Under natural conditions, a great many habits are acquired with a minimum of reinforcement; even more striking is the fact that many habits are highly resistant to extinction under natural conditions. For example, slot machines often are set to pay off at 90 to 10 odds with much longer odds for the jackpot, e.g., 1,500 to 1. Anyone acquainted only with the literature of psychology on continuous reinforcement who observes several devoted gamblers, including players of the "slots," will find it very difficult to explain why extinction of the gambling behavior fails to occur. By recognizing that games of chance involve single or double variable-ratio schedules, it is possible to predict strong resistance to extinction.

Again, if a parent wishes to extinguish an undesirable habit in a child she must arrange a set of contingencies which either (1) result in the reinforcement of an incompatible but desirable response or (2) ensure continuous nonreinforcement until extinction occurs. The amazing persistence of a habit in a child, e.g., saying "damn," even under conditions where aversive control of the response is tried, can sometimes be explained by the presence of an occasional reinforcement. It literally is possible, in effect, for one "yes" or instance of approval to undo a hundred "no's" or instances of disapproval.

From our discussion you will recall that extinction occurs if we fail to _____ a   reinforce
response.

Since not every correct response is reinforced under an intermittent (partial) schedule of reinforcement, the unreinforced responses would constitute _____ trials.   extinction

As one would expect, then, acquisition of a habit is rapid when _____ reinforcement is used.   continuous

Under interval schedules of reinforcement, the organism (does, does not) have control over the   does not
stimulus for responding.

Since the source of S^r is external to the organism under interval schedules, the organism can only estimate when the S^r will occur. If organism A is on an FI 14 schedule, while organism B is on a VI 14 schedule, which will have the greater difficulty in estimating when a reinforcement is to occur? _____   organism B

As the time approaches for the S^r to occur under an interval scale, the rate of response (increases, decreases).   increases

One would expect an organism to be able to anticipate the approximate time of the occurrence of the S^r under a(n) _____   FI
schedule.

not expect

Since the organism cannot estimate accurately the occurrence of the S^r under a VI schedule, you would (expect, not expect) a sharp decrease in the rate of responding following the reinforcement.

VI

FI
anticipating when
 the S^r will occur

○ Thus under a(n) _____ schedule, one would expect the rate of responding during each interval to be steadier than under a(n) _____ schedule because of the difficulty the organism has in _____.

internal

Under ratio schedules, the control of the S^r is (internal, external) because the S^r is dependent upon the organism's responses.

S^r

As a result, under an FR schedule, an organism can estimate when the _____ will occur.

would

It follows then that one (would, would not) expect a decrease in rate of responding following the S^r under an FR schedule.

increase

Because the organism can estimate when the S^r is to occur under an FR schedule, one would expect a(n) (increase, decrease) in responding immediately preceding the S^r.

greater

Under a VR schedule, the organism has (greater, less) difficulty in estimating when the S^r will occur than it has under an FR schedule.

higher and
 steadier rate

Therefore, under a VR schedule, you would expect a relatively (higher and steadier rate, lower and more varied rate) than occurs under an FR schedule.

○ Since training under any partial schedule of reinforcement involves both reinforced and non-reinforced responses, would you expect the organism to have difficulty in determining which responses were to be reinforced? _____

yes (particularly when reinforcement varies around an average)

It is surprising to observe that rather rapid extinction usually occurs following training under a CRF schedule, while relatively _____ extinction often occurs under a partial schedule of reinforcement.

slow

○ Label each statement below with the term or terms (VI, FI, FR, VR, CRF) that describe it best.

_____ 1. Has the *most* rapid rate of acquisition.

CRF

_____ 2. The organism can estimate when the next S^r will occur.

CRF, FI, FR

_____ 3. The rate of responding decreases sharply after the S^r occurs.

FI, FR

_____ 4. Is the least resistant to extinction.

CRF

_____ 5. Resistance to extinction may be great, and the rate of responding is high and steady.

VI, VR

_____ 6. Organism has difficulty in estimating when the S^r will occur.

VR, VI

_____ 7. Rapid increase in responding just prior to the occurrence of the S^r.

FI, FR

One will find that applications of the notion of partial reinforcement are not uncommon in his environment. For example, in the world of work and in education, the incentive systems in common use all imply the beliefs that performance can be maintained and that new habits can be acquired in the absence of a continuous reinforcement schedule. Remuneration for work frequently is made on an interval schedule, such as hourly, daily, weekly, monthly, or annually. Less frequently, remuneration is based on a direct measure of productivity, as in "piecework," an example of a fixed-ratio schedule of providing remuneration. Since fixed-ratio schedules lead to high rates of responding, piecework has an appeal to the employer and initially to the employee as well; however, the history of industrial incentive systems shows that employers have tended to reinforce higher and higher rates of responding, i.e., they have tended to set higher and higher ratios of responses to reinforcement, thereby arousing other, and antagonistic, responses to ratio reinforcement. The rise of bonus incentive systems of payment in which the hourly rate of pay is coupled with a bonus for productivity above a quota appears to be an attempt to combine a fixed-interval and a fixed-ratio schedule of remuneration.

The opportunity to improve formal and informal attempts at training humans and animals by imaginative use of one or more schedules of reinforcement is great. Much more effective and efficient use of the time and resources of a society can be made when those responsible for the behavior of other persons come to recognize and use a variety of schedules of reinforcement in a systematic manner.

Many uses of partial schedules have been made in the laboratory and under natural conditions. Since these schedules tend to generate stable and constant rates of responding, it is possible to study the effects of a wide range of independent variables on rate of response, both during acquisition of a habit and during extinction. For example, the effects of drugs, including stimulants and tranquilizers, have been studied extensively. Selected behaviors of military specialists, such as attending to radar or sonar gear, have been maintained through such schedules for sustained periods. Elaborate environments for the automated teaching of reading to preschool children depend heavily on the importance of partial reinforcement in establishing habits and in maintaining them against extinction. In a very intriguing article, "In Defense of Bird Brains," Herrnstein (1965) summarizes several projects in which instrumentally trained pigeons were used as substitutes for humans in a manufacturing system. In one instance, pigeons were trained to inspect an electronic part for defects in the coat of paint. In another case, the same species was trained to inspect capsules used as containers for drugs. In a third project, pigeons were trained to identify humans in color slides (Herrnstein and Loveland, 1964). In all three cases, the pigeons were as good as or better than humans working on the same tasks. Demonstrations on this order point to the effectiveness of instrumental-training techniques as well as to the potentiality of animal "employees" in repetitive complex tasks requiring inspection or scanning behavior.

SHAPING BEHAVIOR

"Operant conditioning shapes behavior as a sculptor shapes a lump of clay" (Skinner, 1953, p. 91). When it is recalled that for a Skinnerian, responses are said to be emitted by rather than elicited from an organism, it is reasonable to wonder how behavior is modified and controlled. In the paragraphs that follow, attention will be turned to the means for shaping behavior, for establishing discrimination, and for building responses into complex sequences or chains.

Response differentiation and successive approximations

Thus far, little has been said about the procedures used to bring the free operant under control. To take a simple case, how would one proceed to bring the pecking response of a chicken under control? Although a variety of approaches can be used, we will assume that we have a Skinner box of the type described earlier. It has a food delivery mechanism which can be operated by the experimenter or which can be connected to a circuit which will activate the mechanism when a key is depressed. If we place a hungry chicken in the apparatus and sit down to wait until it discovers the relationship between the key and the food tray, we may conclude several hours or days later that chickens are as devoid of intelligence as the folklore claims or that operant training is a myth promulgated for devious purposes. Following this procedure is akin to expecting a young child to learn a verbal response such as "doggie" without arranging for the child to experience the dog and the label for it under conditions appropriate for learning. Presumably, in our society, the child would learn eventually to use the label "doggie" in an appropriate fashion, and presumably, assuming that a chicken can learn to peck a key to obtain food, our chicken will discover that obtaining food in the box is contingent upon pecking the key. By using the *method of successive approximations,* we will find that the training will proceed with greater dispatch; that we can direct the behavior of the organism so that it is able to differentiate the terminal response from the multitude of responses emitted. *Response differentiation* refers to the learning of a particular response class out of the many response classes that could be learned in a particular situation.

Since the chicken is hungry, it will tend to explore the box, pecking at various objects, such as shiny spots, dots of light, bits of feather, and specks of dust. If we place a small quantity of a preferred food such as cracked corn in the food tray, the chicken will soon discover and consume it. Exploration and random pecking will be resumed. Now we shall activate the food mechanism manually, thus releasing a small quantity of food into the food tray; again, our hungry bird will find it and consume it. We may notice that the bird now stays closer to the food tray. The next few times that its head is close to the tray, we trip the mechanism again and soon the attention of the bird will focus on the tray frequently. The key which we wish our subject to peck is located about six inches directly above the food tray and we must find a way to center the bird's attention on the key. For a while, therefore, each time that the bird is facing the key at eye level, we activate the food mechanism; that is, we reinforce those responses of attention to and approach toward the key. As we succeed in shaping this behavior, in differentiating this class of responses from all others occurring, we change the contingencies slightly and reinforce the chicken only when his beak is close to the key. In effect, we systematically shape the behavior of key pecking by reinforcing some remotely related response initially, then by reinforcing successively only those responses which bring the animal closer to the terminal behavior desired, viz., pecking a key. It may have occurred to the reader that this process is not unlike "Twenty Questions" and related games in which a frequent reinforcer is, "No, but you are getting warmer." "Successive approximations," then, refers to shaping a terminal response, the operant level of which is low initially, by systematically reinforcing closer and closer approximations to it.

When a response of greater complexity or on a higher level than a chicken's key pecking must be shaped, successive approximation is applied in the same fashion. Frequently, the objective is to shape complex sequences of behavior rather than a single class of operant;

this topic will be discussed after consideration is given to generalization and discrimination in instrumental learning.

One of the important considerations in learning is for the organism to be able to differentiate between the response which produces a reward and the responses which do not. Since the random behavior of a chicken in a Skinner box might include both the flapping of its wings and a pecking response, it is necessary for the chicken to _____ the response that produces the reward.

differentiate

Whether or not the wing-flapping response, the pecking response, or some other response increases in frequency is dependent upon which _____ is followed closely and consistently by a reinforcing event.

response

Learning a particular response class out of the many response classes which could be learned in a particular situation is called response _____.

differentiation

Thus, learning to peck a disk rather than flapping the wings in a particular situation is an example of _____.

response
  differentiation

The response the experimenter desires the subject to learn is called "terminal behavior." If an experimenter desires that a rat learn to press a bar for food, the bar-pressing response would be considered _____.

terminal
  behavior

Since it is unlikely that an organism will "discover" a desired set of complex terminal behaviors, an experimenter begins to shape behavior by reinforcing approximations to the terminal behavior. If terminal response in an experiment is bar pressing and a rat is presented with a food pellet when it turns in the direction of the bar, what response is an approximation of the terminal response? _____

turning toward
the bar

○ Next, the rat is reinforced only when it walks toward the bar. Then, it is reinforced only when it is close to and facing the bar. List the three successive approximations of the terminal response which were reinforced:

turning toward
the bar

1. _____

walking toward
the bar

2. _____

close proximity
to and facing
the bar

3. _____

successive

Thus, it is possible, by reinforcing a series of _____ approximations to the terminal behavior, for the rat to learn that S^r is contingent upon being close to the bar.

successive
  approximations
behavior
  (response)

When the rat's behavior is shaped through a series of _____ of the terminal _____, it learns to remain in close proximity to the bar.

increased

Because the rat now spends much of its time in the area of the bar, the probability that the bar-pressing response will occur is (increased, decreased).

pressing the bar

During the course of further exploratory behavior, the rat presses the bar and is reinforced. In this example, the terminal behavior was _____.

The terminal behavior of the rat was shaped through the method of _____.

> successive approximations

The behavior was shaped by systematically _____ closer and closer approximations of the _____.

> reinforcing
> terminal behavior

The method of successive approximations refers to _____ the terminal behavior.

> shaping

During the shaping process, one can observe that the organism is emitting (the same response, several similar responses), one of which is reinforced periodically.

> several similar responses

Since several similar responses are emitted during shaping, it is apparent that the organism exhibits _____ generalization.

> response

○ An organism learns a particular response class out of many possible response classes which could have been learned. This is an example of _____.

> response differentiation

○ In operant training, the responses the experimenter desires subjects to learn are called the "_____."

> terminal behaviors

○ The process by which the desired terminal behavior of an organism is brought under control is called "_____."

> shaping

Generalization and discrimination

In shaping behavior, that is, in gaining control over a free operant, it is necessary to recognize that it is a *class* of responses rather than a single response that is shaped. To return for a moment to the chicken that is to learn to peck a key in a situation in which the method of successive approximations is applied, an observer would note that at any stage of approximation to the terminal response desired, the chicken emits responses that are similar, but not identical. In effect, the bird exhibits *response generalization* or a class of similar, related responses.

If the conditions in the apparatus are modified slightly, it also will be apparent that *stimulus generalization* occurs as readily in operant training as it does in classical conditioning. Assume that the key in the Skinner box can be illuminated or not at the discretion of the experimenter. With this modification in the apparatus, light can be used as a discriminative stimulus (S^D), a stimulus which *sets the occasion* for a response and which also can serve to *maintain* a response. To demonstrate this with the chicken, which by now has learned that reinforcement is contingent upon pecking the key, we need only change the contingency to reinforcement when the key is illuminated, no reinforcement when the key is dark. At first, our hungry bird will continue to peck the key indiscriminately; eventually, it will learn that the S^r, food, can be obtained only when the light is on (S^D). When the key is dark, it is a stimulus (S^Δ or S delta) for nonreinforcement.

The distinction between S^D and S^Δ may be made clearer by placing a white light and a green light in the panel in the proximity of the key. The green light could be made an S^D for "time to eat" and the white light an S^Δ for "time to rest" by making S^r contingent upon pecking the key when the green light is present.

By this procedure, conditioned discrimination may be established. It involves essentially the same process of selective reinforcement and nonreinforcement as described for conditioned discrimination in classical conditioning, although in classical conditioning the meaning of reinforcement appears to be quite different. In establishing a conditioned discrimination by Pavlovian training, CS_1 (the green light) is paired with the US (the food), and CS_2 (the white light) is never paired with the US regardless of whether the organism responds correctly from trial to trial. In operant training, the S^r is received only when the animal *emits* the correct response, when it acts on its environment in a manner which produces the consequence S^r.

With a two-light situation, stimulus generalization and stimulus discrimination can be demonstrated readily. Initially, the organism will respond to the key with either light on and, probably, with both lights off. At this stage, many stimuli from the box and from the animal constitute a class of stimuli. After further training, the light on–light off distinction will be acquired. At this stage, the chicken perceives the S^D to be presence or absence of light, regardless of color, form, intensity, etc. Later, it can come to distinguish one light from the other as an S^D for key pecking. If one were interested in testing the bird's ability to discriminate small differences in hue or in saturation, the green light could be shifted gradually toward the white in value until a point was reached at which the discrimination broke down. This technique has been used very effectively to study the sensory capacity and sensory acuity of a number of species. In effect, it is a technique which enables an organism to "indicate" its range and quality of behavior to an investigator on demand (Blough, 1961).

The relationship between response differentiation and stimulus discrimination is a point of considerable significance in understanding the processes underlying the shaping of behavior. To differentiate a class of responses from all other classes of responses, the organism must be able to discriminate the internal stimuli associated with one class and differentiate them from internal stimuli associated with other existing classes of responses. If this were not done, the reinforcing stimulus would be associated with too coarse a group of responses. In a sense, under successive approximations, the organism is learning a conditioned discrimination among *competing* classes of internal stimuli. Again, one can test the discrimination capacity of an organism by determining how fine a response differentiation the subject can make, although response differentiation is a function of other factors than ability to learn discriminations.

Stimulus control of operants can be carried much further than is indicated by the light on–light off and two-light examples. If a hungry and thirsty animal is used, a red light could be added to the white and green lights and used as an S^D for water, an S^r. With higher organisms, such as the human child, several verbal stimuli may be used as S^Ds to control and maintain a series of behaviors simultaneously. For example, a motor skill may be shaped through successive approximations where the control stimuli are verbal stimuli, such as "slow," "fast," "just right," "slower," and "faster," with S^rs of reproof, praise, and knowledge of results.

In most cases, a pigeon conditioned to peck a white disk will also peck a black disk or vice

stimulus
  generalization

versa. From this, it may be concluded that _____ as well as response generalization occurs in operant training.

If, after the pigeon learns to peck a disk for food, whether it be black or white, the organism is reinforced *only* when it pecks the black disk, you would expect the bird to (1) continue to

black

white

peck the _____ key and (2) cease to respond (extinguish) to the _____ key.

Since the color of the keys served as a stimulus

stimulus

(S^D) or signal for the pecking response, it becomes clear that _____ discrimination can be developed through instrumental training.

A stimulus which sets the occasion for a response and which also serves to maintain the response is called a "discriminative stimulus" (S^D). In the

color

previous example, _____ served as the S^D.

food

Although _____ was the S^r which reinforced the pecking of the disk, the

color

_____ of the key *set the occasion* for the response.

○ Thus an S^D not only maintains a response, it

sets the occasion

also _____ for the response.

In the example cited, the stimulus which was not

white

reinforced was _____ (color). A nonreinforced stimulus is called "S^Δ" or "S delta."

The black color which was used to set the

discriminative
  stimulus

occasion for the response is called the "_____" (S^D) while the white color is

called "_____" because it did not S^Δ
serve to set the occasion for the response of disk
pecking.

It is possible to establish conditioned discrimination by _____ responses selectively.   reinforcing

○ Label each statement below with the appropriate term: stimulus discrimination, response
generalization, stimulus generalization, or successive approximations. During instrumental
training in a Skinner box:

_____1. A pigeon learns to peck a   stimulus
                disk for food and it pecks   generalization
                any disk regardless of color.

_____2. A pigeon is reinforced for   successive
                approaching a disk or key   approximations
                which it eventually is to
                peck.

_____3. A pigeon not only pecks the   response
                disk, it may also ruffle its   generalization
                feathers or flap its wings
                regularly.

_____4. The stimulus which sets the S^D
                occasion for making a re-
                sponse.

_____5. An organism learns to press S^D
                a lever for water only when
                a light is on.

Chaining

The process by which a series of responses, habits, or operants are
linked together is known as *chaining*. If we wish to teach our chicken
to perform a more complex set of behaviors before pecking the key,
it is necessary only to select a series of responses or acts of which the
chicken is capable, decide upon an order in which we wish the
responses to occur, and then make the set of responses contingent
upon each other (specifically, making S^r contingent upon key pecking

only if our subject has first turned his back to the key and pecked at the wall opposite to that containing the key). To accomplish this, we would have to establish the habit of turning away from the key and pecking the opposite wall, a habit which would be established through the method of successive approximations. Then this segment would have to be linked to the segment, key pecking. The linking would be done at first with primary reinforcement on a continuous reinforcement schedule, then shifted to an intermittent schedule, and finally shifted to secondary reinforcement, where the reinforcing stimuli would be those produced by the animal's own movements. In teaching complex motor skills, such as dancing to a bear or walking a tightrope to a dog, one can see that a hierarchy of habits has to be acquired and that each habit in the hierarchy is dependent upon the habit which precedes, thus providing a smooth "running-off" of sequential responses which depend upon stimulus discrimination, response differentiation, and reinforcing stimuli—both primary and secondary.

At the human level, the chaining produces long sequences of responses resulting in extraordinarily complex behavior. For example, look at the sequence of behavior required in the simple act of obtaining a gum ball from a machine. Assume that the child has arrived at the machine; then the process in oversimplified form would be:

S^D (gum balls in machine) $\longrightarrow$ R (places penny in slot)
$\longrightarrow$ S^D (hears penny drop into place) $\longrightarrow$ R (pulls lever)
$\longrightarrow$ S^D (sees and hears gum ball fall into receptacle)
$\longrightarrow$ R (removes gum ball from machine) $\longrightarrow$ S^D (feels and sees gum ball in hand) $\longrightarrow$ R (places gum ball in mouth)
$\longrightarrow$ S^r (sweet taste, etc.)

This type of analysis, a *functional analysis of behavior,* may be made for any complex series of responses, such as dancing, writing, playing a piano, playing tennis, or reading, by determining the successful terminal act and then systematically answering the question, step by step backward through the chain, *What are the variables of which this behavior is a function?* Once an analysis has been made, it may be possible to improve the training procedures which are used in teaching a particular skill.

Significant steps have been made in the development of a technology of learning by Skinner and his colleagues. Through careful programing of the components of a task, where the components have been identified through a functional analysis, the teaching of such subjects and skills as reading, writing, and typing has been improved significantly. The development of teaching machines and programed instruction in recent years also originated in Skinner's laboratory (for example, see Skinner, 1954; Holland, 1959). Other extensions of instrumental-training procedures have been made to a wide range of animal and human behavior. Turkeys have been trained to play shuffleboard and hens to play a primitive form of baseball. Pigeons have played ping pong, and pigs have operated vacuum cleaners while walking on their hind legs—complete with aprons. Severely disturbed mental patients have regained sufficient contact with reality to respond to conventional treatment such as psychotherapy. Air crews have been trained to remain alert, to sustain attention to monotonous stimulation, and to respond to complex discriminative stimuli with equally complex behavior.

Chaining is the process by which a series of habits, responses, or operants are linked together. Assume that if a rat is to obtain food (S^r), he must first jump up on a platform, then press bar A and bar B, in order, when a light is on. The three responses must be linked or _____ together.	chained
In this example, the rat first learned to _____ between responses through reinforcement of those behaviors which approximated the terminal behavior.	differentiate (discriminate)
_____ differentiation then becomes an important first step in chaining.	Response
The rat also learned to press bar B after leaping to the platform only if a light was on. This would be an example of responding to a _____ stimulus.	discriminative (S^D)

108

○ Thus, to shape the behavior of this rat, the experimenter must give attention first to the concept of response _____, next to _____ (pressing the bar only when

differentiation
stimulus
  discrimination
chaining

the light is on), and finally, to _____ these responses together.

○ The process of linking responses together, _____, becomes an important activity in _____ the behavior of an organism.

chaining
shaping

○ A dog learns that in order to obtain food it must bark, jump up on a platform, and sit on its hind legs, in that order. The process by which the dog learns this series of responses is called

chaining

_____.

○ The shaping process necessary to successful chaining of the behavior mentioned in the preceding frame includes three major concepts. They are:

response
  differentiation

1. _____

stimulus
  discrimination

2. _____

chaining

3. _____

ESCAPE AND AVOIDANCE CONDITIONING

If we return to the Skinner box and utilize the grid floor through which electric shock can be administered to the feet of an organism such as a rat, cat, or a dog, we shall be able to examine some of the phenomena of instrumental learning when the reinforcing event is negative rather than positive. A *negative reinforcing stimulus* is one which strengthens an operant by its termination, i.e., by the removal of the S^r. We shall consider (1) learning to *escape,* (2) learning to *avoid* aversive stimulation, and briefly (3) the topic of punishment.

If we place an untrained rat in the box and turn on the shock, the animal will actively seek to escape from the noxious stimulus through leaping and crouching. In the process, one of its movements will result in depressing the lever in the box which will turn off the shock rather than deliver food or water. Thus, the task to be learned is that termination of the noxious stimulus is contingent upon pressing the lever. Learning this task is called *escape conditioning* because pressing the lever is instrumental in escaping the stimulus. Thus, any behavior which is acquired through termination of aversive stimulation can be referred to as escape conditioning.

At the human level the learning of mechanisms for escape from other people is not uncommon because the actions of persons as well as the actions of things sometimes are aversive. If the person discovers a means of terminating the aversive stimulation arising from other persons, the probability is great that he will use that means when he next experiences similar stimulation. Thus, children frequently learn early that they can escape some parental demands through daydreams and fantasy. In some cases this mode of dealing with the demands of adults may become so well established that it persists into adulthood, often in a pathological form. One well-known writer of exotic "escape fiction," for example, was discovered by a literary agent who found that the writer was in the habit of constructing elaborate fantasies which he repeated to himself aloud. Schizophrenic behavior might be viewed, within this frame of reference, as an elaborate hierarchy of habits for escape. For some people, the migratory nature of such occupations as carnival and circus work, seafaring, and selling provides a means of escape from some of the aversive characteristics of membership in primary social groups. At this level, it is probably evident that several operants have been shaped into "styles of life" through response differentiation, stimulus discrimination, and chaining.

Extinction trials for escape behavior tend to produce the same orderly results which are found for the typical habit acquired under positive continuous reinforcement; that is, extinction is quite rapid. In escape training, the noxious stimulus occurs without warning, that is, without an S^D. If the S^r is termination of a noxious stimulus, one would suppose that absence of the stimulus would result in failure to try to escape, and this is the case in pure escape learning. However, if the situation in which the escape training occurs contains distinctive cues which come to have secondary reinforcing properties, an organism may continue to escape if this alternative is available.

Returning to the animal laboratory and the Skinner box, we may examine aversive conditioning further. At this point, we add an S^D to the situation to discover whether the organism can learn to depress the lever when a light is turned on as a signal that shock will occur in two seconds unless the lever is depressed. The situation described is that for *avoidance conditioning.* Note that in this situation, the subject will not be shocked on every trial as was the case in escape conditioning; instead, when it learns that light is an S^D for the response of lever pressing, it can avoid the shock on every trial simply by responding to the lever within two seconds. Thus, in escape conditioning, the organism *terminates* the aversive stimulus by an appropriate response, while in avoidance conditioning, it *prevents* the occurrence of the aversive stimulus by an appropriate response.

The Skinner box is not as effective a piece of apparatus for demonstrating avoidance learning as is a shuttlebox, which consists of two compartments separated by a door or gate (Fig. 5). When one or more stimuli (S^Ds) are present and when their presence signals the coming of a noxious stimulus which can be prevented by responding, the conditions are set for avoidance learning. If a light is used as an S^D in the shuttlebox to signal that shock will occur in two seconds and if the organism has an opportunity to avoid the shock by running into another compartment, it will soon learn to avoid shock on all trials.

An interesting question to be considered is the nature of the reinforcing event in avoidance conditioning. Given the paradigm of operant learning, one would predict that the nonoccurrence of shock on trial after trial would result in extinction, not in the maintenance of the avoidance habit. Yet, if one observes what happens, he discovers that extinction does not always occur; instead, after the rat learns to avoid the shock for a few trials, it is a more reliable avoider than ever. Thus, by definition, avoidance of the shock seems to have strengthened the rat's behavior. *Avoiding the shock seems to have strengthened that act which led to its avoidance.* To extinguish this habit, one would suppose that turning off the shock would lead to longer and longer latency of the running response until the animal would no longer avoid the compartment when the light was turned on. *Sometimes,* very rapid extinction of avoidance responses occurs. On

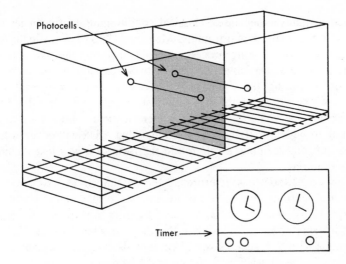

Fig. 5 Shuttlebox for escape and avoidance conditioning. Shock is applied from the grid floor through the feet of the animal. When the animal moves close to the gate, the photocell is activated and the gate is raised electrically, permitting the animal to escape into the adjoining compartment.

the other hand, in several studies tremendous resistance to extinction has been produced. Using dogs as subjects, Solomon et al. (1953) found that not only did extinction fail to occur in some animals following hundreds of no-shock trials, but also the latencies of the response of jumping from one compartment to another in a shuttlebox actually improved in the *absence of shock*. How can one explain the paradox of obtaining improvement in a habit, instead of extinction, in the absence of the S^r?

Most theorists have dealt with this issue by postulating *fear reduction* or *anxiety reduction* as the S^r. They have argued that the S^D, in this case the light, is really a conditioned stimulus for fear and the shock is an unconditioned stimulus for fear; hence, in the early training trials for a naïve subject, a classical conditioned response is formed in which some stimulus comes to control a fear or anxiety response. In the situation at hand, the onset of the light (a CS for fear and an S^D for avoidance conditioning) arouses fear which is terminated by running to the safe compartment; thus, the S^r is said to be fear or anxiety reduction, not avoidance of shock. In this case and, in fact, in many other cases, classical conditioning contingencies are built into the instrumental training. Mowrer (1960) has distinguished the classical conditioning process as problem-posing and the operant learning process as problem-solving, a two-factor theory of learning. In problem posing, the organism is confronted with new motivational factors which he solves through new instrumental acts. Another way of phrasing the dichotomy is to consider classical conditioning to be learning in which a *sign,* the CS, signifies that a US will occur, while in instrumental training, a *solution* in the form of a new instrumental act is required.

Mowrer (1960) has interpreted the resistance to extinction in avoidance learning as a failure of the animal to discriminate between "in-apparatus" and "out-of-apparatus" training to respond to signals. This interpretation assumes that the dog associates the S^D in the apparatus with S^Ds, such as verbal commands, which it receives when it is outside the shuttlebox. Solomon and Wynne (1954), on the other hand, suggest that the dogs in their shuttlebox studies failed to extinguish the habit of jumping the barrier to avoid shock because during training the jumping not only avoided shock, it also reduced fear. Because most dogs responded to the fear-producing stimulus (the light) *very rapidly,* they tended to maintain their anxiety or fear intact and failed to discover that the contingencies in the situation had been changed.

The discovery that classical conditioning contingencies and instrumental-training contingencies are interrelated has led to promising research on the nature of these interrelationships. For example, studies of autonomic conditioning (classical conditioning) have been combined with studies of instrumental avoidance training following the discovery that heart rate was changed during the early trials of avoidance conditioning. In the next few years, it can be expected that the nature of the interrelationships will be clarified and that extensions to some types of human behavior, particularly to neurotic behaviors, will have been made.

The notion of fear or anxiety reduction as the S^r for avoidance behavior is very attractive, since the concept of anxiety has been used widely by personality and motivation theorists with little support for the concept from the work of the experimentalists, although with considerable support from clinical practice. That humans learn to avoid is evident, but what motivates them, i.e., what reinforces them for avoiding, has been largely a matter for conjecture. One might suppose that some avoidance behavior in the human is acquired through much the same process as is found in the animal laboratory. For example, how do words (S^Ds) come to exert such control over behavior? Why does a specific statement such as "You are bad" or "That is bad" produce essentially the same general reaction in every American child? In many families during childhood, the individual receives aversive stimulation for some of the operants emitted. If the operant is followed by an aversive S^r, the result may be (1) to strengthen the operant or to increase the probability of its occurrence in the future, (2) to inhibit or depress the operant (punishment), or (3) to remove the S^r (to escape). If "You are bad" is used as an S^D, and spanking and shouting of the phrase are the aversive S^rs, the situation is set for the development of conditioned fear and for avoidance behavior. If the aversive stimuli continue to occur each time the operant occurs or *even on an intermittent schedule of reinforcement,* the child may soon learn to avoid the S^rs of spanking and shouting by preventing their occurrence with an apology (for example, "I didn't mean to do it"), with denial (for example, "I didn't do it; Ted did"), with aggression, tantrums, etc. If the S^D "You are bad," accompanied by the same and other S^rs, occurs in conjunction with a wide variety of operants emitted by the child, he may come to avoid the adult, that is, "turn off" the adult through one or more habitually used defense mechanisms. If several other persons tell him "You are bad," he might develop apprehension or anxiety of social contacts with any person and he might even come to think of himself as "a bad person," thus generating feelings of guilt about many of his acts.

Just as an animal can learn to press a bar or make some other appropriate response to gain a reward, it can also be conditioned to make an appropriate response to _____ or   avoid
_____ _____ something which is painful or   escape
distasteful.

A dog that is being shocked steps on a pedal that turns off the shock. The dog learns quickly

stepping on
a pedal
removal
(termination)

to step on the pedal to escape the aversive stimulus. In this example, the response learned is _____, the S^r is _____ of the electric shock.

terminate (avoid
or escape)
negative

If food is used as an S^r, the animal works to obtain the food which serves as a positive reinforcer. When a painful or noxious stimulus is used, the animal works to _____ the stimulus. A noxious stimulus is a _____ reinforcer.

positive
negative

Both _____ and _____ reinforcers may be used to strengthen operants, the negative reinforcer by its termination and the positive S^r by its receipt.

removal

"Escape conditioning" refers to any strengthening of behavior which comes about through the (addition, removal) of aversive stimulation.

S^D

bell

If shock occurs regularly following the ringing of a bell for 30 seconds, the bell is an _____ which sets the occasion for an organism to avoid the shock by responding to the _____.

negative (painful)
S^D

Thus, in avoidance conditioning, the subject may avoid the _____ stimulus by responding appropriately to an _____.

escape

prevent

Avoidance and escape conditioning differ in that under escape-conditioning training, an appropriate response makes possible only an _____ from the negative stimulus, while under avoidance conditioning, an appropriate response makes it possible for the subject to _____ the noxious stimulus from occurring.

A rat trained to press a bar in response to an
S^D, to prevent the occurrence of an aversive
stimulus, will be more resistant to _____   extinction
than a rat trained to press a bar in response to
an S^D to obtain (positive, negative) reinforce-   positive
ment.

For extinction to occur, the organism must per-
ceive that the *contingency* between response
and reinforcer has been changed. In avoidance
conditioning, the organism responds to the S^D to
prevent the noxious stimulus; therefore, during
extinction trials the organism may not discover
the change in the _____ between   contingency
response and reinforcer.

Under avoidance conditioning, the organism
may be unable to discover the change in contingency because the response to the S^D
_____ the occurrence of the aversive   prevents
stimulus.

Only if the organism fails to respond to the
_____ can it discover that the aver- S^D
sive stimulus no longer occurs.

○ Some theorists have proposed that a link
between classical conditioning and instrumental
training can easily be shown in avoidance conditioning. The classical CR in avoidance conditioning is thought to be a conditioned
_____ response.   fear

According to these theorists, the organism, by
running, jumping, etc., not only avoids the aversive stimulus but also reduces _____.   fear (anxiety)

Recent research seems to support the notion   instrumental
that Pavlovian contingencies probably are pres-   (operant,
ent in every case of _____ learning.   avoidance)

escape

To this point, we have discussed aversive stimuli in connection with avoidance and _____ conditioning. They also are used in punishment, which may be thought of as passive avoidance training.

PUNISHMENT

Before leaving the topic of aversive stimulation, it is necessary to consider briefly the matter of *punishment,* the use of aversive stimuli to prevent the occurrence of behavior. Specifically, "A punishment is a noxious stimulus, one which will support, by its termination or omission, the growth of new escape or avoidance responses. It is one which the subject will reject, if given a choice between the punishment and no stimulus at all" (Solomon, 1964, p. 239). In neither escape training nor *active* avoidance training, described above, is the goal of the experimenter that of inhibiting a response. In punishment training, however, suppression is the goal, not escape from or avoidance of stimuli. The human use of punishment as a technique of individual and social control has its roots in antiquity; yet, it is surprising to discover that little sound information exists on the effects of punishment on behavior. Further, results from laboratory studies on punishment have produced some very confusing results.

Solomon (1964) categorizes studies of punishment as follows:

1. Studies in which behavior acquired under positive S^rs is punished, for example, punishing the key-pecking response or the lever-pressing response of subjects who have acquired these responses through instrumental training with food or water as the S^r.
2. Studies in which behavior acquired under negative reinforcement is punished, for example, punishing an individual for observing a social taboo such as the nonuse of profanity.
3. Studies in which innate consummatory behavior is punished, for example, punishing a higher organism during copulation or punishing a thirsty organism for drinking.
4. Studies in which instinctive behavior is punished, for example, punishing a turkey for emitting his elaborate courtship pattern or punishing a male dog for demarcating his territory with urine.

5. Studies in which a reflex is punished, for example, punishing micturition in a dog or the eyeblink reflex in a human.

At least one important generalization can be drawn from these studies—that the effects of punishing stimuli have meaning only within the context of (1) the animal's nature, (2) its history of experience, (3) the characteristics of the stimulus, and (4) the nature of the situation in which the punishment is applied, including the events which precede and follow the application of the stimulus. Thus, parents' persistent question of whether to punish or not to punish their children cannot be answered simply, if at all, without knowing a great deal about the previous history of reinforcement associated with the behavior to be punished, the nature of the aversive stimulus to be used, the strength of the response to be punished, and the conditions existing at the time the punishing stimulus is applied, plus knowledge of several lesser factors. If these conditions are not specified or cannot be specified, one cannot predict accurately whether the use of an aversive stimulus will increase, decrease, or suppress the response in question. Studies of punishment have produced all three of these effects plus others. For example, if one applies mild punishment during the course of habit *acquisition* under positive reinforcement, the punishing stimulus may become a positive secondary reinforcing stimulus, an S^r as it were, and its presence may lead to an increased frequency of responding. On the other hand, mild aversive stimulation may result in an increase in the variability of behavior, which then causes the learning of an alternative response, providing that alternatives are available. On the other hand, if a very intense aversive stimulus is applied in the same situation, suppression of the response may occur. If intense punishment is applied to a consummatory response such as eating, the effects may be dramatic in that starvation may occur. This is particularly likely to happen if the temporal order of events is such that punishment is applied *immediately preceding* the consumption of food. Still other effects are obtained when instinctive behavior and reflex behavior are punished or when the qualities of the stimulus are varied. Intense stimulation may produce fear, anxiety, and neurotic behavior, particularly if no alternative means of problem solving are provided.

It seems evident, then, that the topic of the effects of punishment

118

deserves more thorough investigation, particularly at the human level. Until a solid body of empirically determined data has been developed, the effects on individual behavior of laws, spankings, threats, capital punishment, incarceration, and other aversive stimuli will continue to produce unpredictable results.

aversive

Punishment is the use of _____ stimuli to *prevent* the occurrence of behavior.

punishment

If a hungry organism is shocked each time it begins to eat, the aversive stimulus (shock) would be used as _____.

learning

response

In both escape and active avoidance training the goal of the experimenter is the _____ of a response, while in punishment (passive avoidance training) the goal is the suppression (or inhibition) of a _____.

suppressed
(inhibited)

If a hungry dog were shocked each time it began to eat, one would expect that the eating response would be _____.

aversive

A careful analysis of studies of punishment indicates that the effects of punishment are extremely varied. In most instances, the _____ stimuli used as punishment suppress behavior; however, in other instances, they may increase the rate of responding.

suppresses

Whether punishment _____, increases, or decreases a response is contingent on a number of factors, including the animal's nature and its history of experience.

would not

One (would, would not) expect punishment to have the same effect on a horse with a docile disposition as on a horse with a nervous disposition.

In an attempt to predict the effects of punishment on an organism's response, one needs to know, in addition to the animal's _____, (1) its _____, (2) the characteristics of the stimulus, and (3) the nature of the situation in which the punishment is applied.

nature
history of
   experience

○ Name the four conditions which must be considered if the effects of punishing stimuli are to have meaning:

1. _____

animal's nature

2. _____

history of
   experience

3. _____

characteristics of
   the stimulus

4. _____

nature of the
   situation

○ Label each item below with the term or terms most nearly related to it—escape conditioning, avoidance conditioning, punishment.

_____1. The termination of an aversive stimulus.

escape
   conditioning

_____2. A response makes possible the prevention of the noxious stimulus.

avoidance
   conditioning

_____3. The stimulus is designed to suppress a response.

punishment

_____4. The use of an aversive stimulus.

escape
   conditioning,
avoidance
   conditioning,
punishment

escape
  conditioning

_____5. Termination of the aversive stimulus provides reinforcement.

punishment

_____6. The response to the noxious stimulus is frequently unpredictable.

escape
  conditioning

_____7. Extinction trials produce results similar to those habits acquired under continuous reinforcement.

avoidance
  conditioning

_____8. May be highly resistant to extinction.

punishment

_____9. Each time a thirsty rat begins to drink an aversive stimulus is applied.

References

Boyd, B. O., and Warren, J. M. Solution of oddity problems by cats. *J. Comp. Physiol. Psychol.*, 1957, **50**, 258–260.

Ferster, C. B., and Skinner, B. F. Schedules of reinforcement. New York: Appleton-Century-Crofts, 1957.

Moon, L. E., and Harlow, H. F. Analysis of oddity learning by monkeys. *J. Comp. Physiol. Psychol.*, 1955, **48**, 188–194.

Porter, D. A critical review of a portion of the literature on teaching devices. *Harvard Educ. Rev.*, 1957, **27**, 126–147.

Warren, J. M. Oddity learning set in a cat. *J. Comp. Physiol. Psychol.*, 1960, **53**, 433–434.

Wodinsky, J., and Bitterman, M. E. The solution of oddity-problems by the rat. *Amer. J. Psychol.*, 1953, **66**, 137–140.

4

Variables Affecting Conditioning

One aim of the student of the processes of learning is to determine the antecedents (i.e., the independent variables) that affect or bring about changes in the measures of behavior (the dependent variables) he uses. In the preceding sections, several independent and dependent variables were discussed, and the relationship between some of them was noted. Several of the important relationships that facilitate or retard conditioning are presented in this section for purposes of review and clarification. In a sense, these principles constitute a prescription, the do's and don't's, for success in utilizing conditioning techniques, although the prescription is sufficiently incomplete to make accurate prediction of the outcome hazardous at times.

Accurate predictions of outcomes still are difficult because (1) several variables involved in conditioning and extinction require additional study, (2) in many cases, the studies upon which generalizations are based fail to distinguish between learning and performance, and (3) several different measures of learning, i.e., dependent variables, have been used by investigators, resulting at times in conflicting conclusions. As was noted earlier, the design of research which separates learning variables and performance variables is very difficult, at times impossible. As a consequence, some of the factors discussed below, particularly those related to the parameters of reinforcement, probably are essentially performance variables. Of course, if one's interest is in changing behavior by manipulating one or more independent variables, his interest is in performance, that is, terminal responses. The theorist is more likely to be concerned with pure learning than is the specialist in training.

The less-than-perfect agreement among measures of learning is not surprising since they reflect somewhat different classes of performance, classes which presumably are affected differentially by at least some of the performance variables. When resistance to extinction is used as a measure of the acquisition of a habit, differences found among studies of the same phenomenon may be a function of variables which influence extinction (retention) but not learning.

With these limitations in mind, consideration now will be given to a number of variables. An attempt has been made to place the variables in a few classes for purposes of discussion and to facilitate learning.

REINFORCEMENT VARIABLES (US AND S^r)

Practice

The relationship between the number of reinforced trials and the strength of a habit generally has been found to be positive and direct. Thus, the strength of a classical CR or the rate of response in operant learning increases as a function of the number of reinforced trials, other factors being equal.

Nonreinforcement

The effect of nonreinforcement is a gradual decrease in the strength of a habit or in rate of response; that is, extinction occurs, other factors being equal. When resistance to extinction is used as a measure of learning, the rate of extinction may be affected by such variables as the schedule of reinforcement during acquisition, the degree of similarity between acquisition and extinction conditions (the more similar the conditions, the slower is the extinction), and the number of competing responses present.

Partial reinforcement

We have found that acquisition rates vary as a function of the schedule of reinforcement used, and that continuous reinforcement is most effective for acquisition. However, it has also been shown that if retention is of primary importance, partial reinforcement schedules are superior since maximum resistance to extinction can be obtained by using variable schedules of reinforcement.

Quantity of reinforcement

In general, results support the generalization that strength of response is greater for large quantities than for small quantities of reinforcement. Quantity of reinforcement probably is a performance variable, one that falls within the class "incentive motivation."

Quality of reinforcement

Again, differential rates of response have been obtained by varying the quality, i.e., the hedonic value, of the reinforcer. Again, the perceived value of a reinforcing stimulus is closely related to motivation for learning. Receipt of a grade for a composition is not likely to be perceived in the same manner and to have the same effect on later composition writing as receipt of $50 instead of an A, $30 instead of a B, and so on down to a $50 fine for an F. Receipt of candy for each correct response probably will not affect the rate of responding in a two-year-old child in the same manner as receipt of a penny for each correct response.

Conditioned reinforcers

The presence or absence of positive secondary reinforcing stimuli either during acquisition or during extinction can affect the strength of a response or the rate of responding. Supplementing the primary S^r or US with secondary reinforcement may have the effect of enriching and stabilizing the situation in which reinforcement occurs, thus helping to maintain response strength until primary reinforcement occurs. When resistance to extinction is used as a measure of learning, recognition needs to be given to the finding that the presence of secondary reinforcement during extinction trials may retard extinction. When one is working with negative reinforcers, the effects are less clear.

Delay of reinforcement

The rate of responding and the strength of a response may be influenced by the temporal interval between response and reinforcement. In general, the longer the delay, the slower is the conditioning, and trace conditioning is the slowest of all. Again, somewhat different effects are found for operant learning than for classical conditioning and for positive S^rs than for negative S^rs.

animal B

The relationship between the number of reinforced trials and the strength of a habit is generally positive and direct. If animal A receives twenty reinforced trials and animal B receives thirty reinforced trials, habit strength will be greater in which animal? _____

positive
direct

In a maze-learning task, group A receives sixteen reinforced trials and group B receives forty reinforced trials in the maze. It is found that group B makes fewer errors than group A. These results indicate that the relationship between the number of reinforced trials and the strength of a habit is generally _____ and _____.

Rate is decreased
and extinction
occurs.

○ What is the effect on rate of responding or habit strength of nonreinforcement?

_____

more

○ One would expect a VI schedule of reinforcement to be (more, less) resistant to extinction than a continuous-reinforcement schedule.

schedules

Thus, when extinction is used as a measure of learning, one must consider such factors as the _____ of reinforcement used during acquisition.

○ It has been noted that the greater the similarity between extinction and acquisition conditions, the slower is the extinction. If the extinction trials for group A are conducted in the same apparatus and setting that were used in the acquisition of the response, while the extinction trials for group B are conducted in a setting that differs significantly from the one in which the response was acquired, which group would you expect to extinguish most rapidly? _____ Why?
_____

group B
Extinction is most rapid when experimental conditions for extinction differ from those for acquisition.

○ If one were concerned about the *rate* of acquisition, a _____ schedule of reinforcement would be more effective than a partial schedule. On the other hand, a _____ schedule is superior to a continuous schedule in increasing resistance to extinction.

continuous

partial (intermittent)

○ The schedule of partial reinforcement that provides the greatest resistance to extinction is the (variable, fixed) ratio.

variable

○ Generally, the strength of the response is greater for _____ quantities than for smaller quantities of reinforcement.

larger

The strength of a response is often a function of the quality of a reinforcer. A child who works harder when candy is the reward than when a quality

piece of bread is the reward is demonstrating the effects of the _____ of a reinforcer.

○ Another variable that must be considered when using either rate of acquisition or rate of extinction as a measure of learning is whether a secondary reinforcer is present. You would expect a pigeon to extinguish (more rapidly, more slowly) when a clicking sound is heard each time the disk is pecked.

more slowly

○ When using strength of response as a measure of acquisition or retention, one must consider also whether the reinforcer used is positive or _____, whether the approach to conditioning is classical or _____, and whether the interval between response and reinforcement is immediate or _____.

negative
operant
  (instrumental)
delayed

shorter

○ You would expect that the (greater, shorter) the interval of time between reinforcement and response, the more rapid would be the acquisition of a habit.

○ True or false: Place T or F before each of the following:

T

_____1. The greater the number of reinforced trials, the stronger is the habit.

F

_____2. A response learned under a fixed-interval schedule of reinforcement is more resistant to extinction than one learned under a variable-interval schedule.

F

_____3. The greater the disparity in conditions of acquisition and

extinction, the slower is the
extinction.

_____4. Resistance to extinction can   T
be used as a measure of
learning.

_____5. If an experimenter wished to   T
increase the rate of re-
sponding, he might consider
increasing the quantity of
the reinforcement.

_____6. Although quantity of rein-   F
forcement tends to be re-
lated to learning, the quality of the reinforcement
does not.

○ What effect does delay of reinforcement
have on conditioning?   causes a generally
                                                          slower rate
_____

○ Name five reinforcement variables which
may affect rate of responding.

 1. _____

 2. _____

 3. _____

 4. _____

 5. _____

STIMULUS VARIABLES (CS AND S^D)

Intensity

The relative intensity of a conditioning stimulus is intimately related to rate of conditioning in animal subjects, but the findings on the
effects on humans are equivocal. It is reasonable to suppose that one
role of intensity is to influence the ease of discrimination of the stimulus; that is, a stimulus which is well above threshold should stand
out from and contrast with its background.

Attention should also be given to the stimulus-intensity variable
when the conditioning stimulus is to be used as a conditioned rein-

forcer, particularly in escape or avoidance conditioning or in punishment. In the case of punishment (passive avoidance learning), varying the intensity of a conditioned, aversive S^r may result in increased, decreased, or no response.

Duration

Little attention has been given directly to the duration of the CS or S^D although it could affect rate of conditioning through its effects on the process of discrimination. Duration and intensity seemingly would interact in such a manner that a stimulus of low intensity would require a longer duration than a stimulus of high intensity.

Temporal relationship to US and S^r

The temporal relationship between the CS and the US is a variable of critical importance in classical conditioning, and the optimum relationship is CS $\longrightarrow$ US, with a temporal interval between them of one second or less. Lengthening the interval or reversing the order of the stimuli results in slower conditioning or in no conditioning. The temporal relationship of an S^D to an S^r is an important variable, since immediate reinforcement of correct responses results in more rapid acquisition than occurs when reinforcement is delayed. The relationship between the conditioning stimulus and the US and between the S^D and the S^r clearly is affected by delay of reinforcement.

Stimulus complexity

When the stimuli used in conditioning studies are more complex than tone, light, or color, the rate of conditioning may be affected. If the stimulus contains several compatible elements, learning may be facilitated because of the increased possibility of generalization among stimulus elements. On the other hand, if the elements of a complex stimulus tend to conflict among themselves less than they do with background stimuli, conditioning may be slower because of the inhibitory effects of such distractors and the difficulty in discriminating the presence or absence of the stimulus.

○ The rate of conditioning is related to the relative intensity of a CS. One would expect the rate of acquisition of a CR to be greater for a

tone (CS) of (higher, lower) intensity than for   higher
a tone of (higher, lower) intensity.   lower

○ Would you expect a direct relationship to
exist between the rate of responding and the
relative intensity of an S^D? _____   yes

Another stimulus variable which may relate to
the strength of the response is the duration of
the CS or S^D. All other things being equal, it
seems reasonable to assume that under some
conditions, a CS with a duration of two seconds
would have a (greater, lesser) effect on be-   greater
havior than would a CS with a duration of half a
second.

If light ⟶ shock are paired in one study and
shock ⟶ light in another, the subjects in the
shock ⟶ light study will learn a motor task,
e.g., withdrawal of the finger from a key (less,
if at all; more) rapidly than the subjects in the   less, if at all
light ⟶ shock group.

○ From earlier discussion, we know also that
the _____ of the interval between   length
the US and the CS affects the rate of learning.

On the other hand, the temporal relations,
specified above, which are of importance in
classical conditioning, namely, _____   length of interval
and _____, are not as critical when   order of stimuli
one is concerned with the temporal relationship
of an S^D to an S^r.

○ Intensity and duration are examples of
_____ variables which may affect the   stimulus
rate of conditioning.

CS $\longrightarrow$ US
one

○ In classical conditioning, the optimal relationship between the pair of stimuli is _____, and the optimal temporal relationship between them is usually _____ second(s) or less.

compatible

difficulty

○ Rate of conditioning may be increased if the stimuli are (compatible, incompatible). On the other hand, you would expect (ease, difficulty) in discriminating the presence or absence of a stimulus if the elements of a complex stimulus tended to conflict.

compatible
conflict

○ Rate of conditioning as a function of stimulus complexity is enhanced if the stimuli are _____, and inhibited if the stimuli tend to _____.

ORGANISMIC VARIABLES

Variables arising within the organism sometimes serve as independent variables in studies of learning, and occasionally as dependent variables. Quite often they are held constant by means of an experimental design or by statistical techniques such as matching subjects, random assignment of subjects to experimental groups, or using subjects as their own controls. Since these variables may affect the rate of responding or habit strength as measured, they need to be taken into consideration. *Age* and *sex* of the organism can influence the rate of conditioning. Of the two, age is far more likely to interact with learning. When age and sex are significantly related to strength of a habit, it is likely that their influence operates on performance rather than learning. For example, young animals and old animals may require a longer time to run a maze or make a response.

Effort and *frustration* have been shown to be related to acquisition as well as to extinction in complex ways. An increase in effort, such as a requirement that the organism climb a barrier, may enhance the perception of an S^D and hence may serve to facilitate acquisition. On the other hand, the amount of effort required may be so great as to induce fatigue or excessive variability arising from attempts to find alternative means to a goal. *Competing responses,* which may be produced by variation in external as well as in internal stimuli, tend to retard conditioning. The role of competing responses is particularly evident in shaping behavior through the method of successive approximations.

Although it may seem obvious, attention is called to the *past history* of the organism as a variable. In research, this complex variable usually is controlled by using naïve subjects which have been reared under similar conditions or by using subjects as their own experimental control. When the learning processes in humans are under investigation, it is more difficult to meet the assumption that all have had equal experience in learning. Research on learning sets—learning how to learn—and on perceptually or culturally impoverished environments indicates that rates of learning can vary as a function of subtle differences in previous experience with other tasks than the one to be learned. It was noted earlier that the effects of a punishing stimulus may vary as a function of the context in which it is applied, including the events immediately preceding and following the application of the stimulus. It is not unlikely that previous experience with CSs, S^Ds, USs, and S^rs will be shown to fit a generalization similar to that derived from the research on punishment. It may be desirable to distinguish between the *immediate past* and the *remote past* when specifying the conditions for optimum learning—particularly in considering the reinforcement history of an organism.

Level of motivation (drive strength), within limits, has been shown to have a marked facilitative effect on performance, and some learning theorists argue that motivation also enters into learning. Hull (1943) for example, argued that the strength of a habit was a function of the number of reinforced trials, a position which has been very influential in contemporary research on animal learning. When motivation approximates zero, little or no learning is *demonstrated,* i.e., measurable, while at moderate levels of motivation, performance is facilitated. Very high levels of motivation, particularly of fear or anxiety, may retard learning. It should be noted that the effects of motivational variables are more evident in instrumental learning than in classical conditioning because of the importance of active responding—the emission of responses, in instrumental training.

Variation in *physiological states* of the organism may affect rate of conditioning. Naturally enough, momentary variations in the internal states of an organism frequently result in momentary variations in motivation and hence in variations in performance. A large research literature exists on altered physiological states induced by fatigue, stress, drugs, surgical assault, dietary deficiencies, etc. A wide variety of such specific factors have been found to facilitate or retard learning, particularly instrumental learning. Most of the factors appear to exert their influence on performance; hence, they are reflected in measures of learning.

Species and *genetic* differences also influence rate of learning, and studies of these differences constitute the basis for a comparative psychology of learning in which the most frequently used organisms have been fish, pigeons, rats, rhesus monkeys, chimpanzees, and the human child.

organismic	○ In order to have confidence in conclusions concerning the influence of variables external to the organism on learning, one must control for the possible effects of _____ variables.
would effort organismic	If bar pressing is the terminal behavior desired, you (would, would not) expect the rate of bar pressing to depend in part on how much effort is required to depress the bar. It is apparent that _____ can be an _____ variable.
different rates than	The past history of the organism can affect learning. Animals which have been used in several maze-learning studies, for example, may learn at (the same rates as, different rates than) naïve subjects.
immediate	○ When considering the relationship of the history of an organism to learning, it is often important to distinguish between the remote past and the _____ past.

Motivation is another organismic variable which affects learning. A _____ dog has greater motivation and may learn at a greater rate (using food as the S') than a satiated dog.

hungry (deprived)

○ Some of the organismic variables affecting learning are (1) _____, (2) sex, (3) effort, (4) _____, (5) _____ and _____ history, and (6) _____.

age
frustration
immediate
remote
motivation

The physiological state of an organism may influence learning. An animal that has been drugged heavily has a different _____ state than one which is free of drugs.

physiological

○ The social behavior of Rhode Island Red chickens has been observed to be different from that of Leghorn chickens. Thus, _____ differences also influence rate of learning.

species

○ Name four of the organismic variables which frequently affect learning.

1. _____

age and sex

2. _____

effort and
    frustration

3. _____

competing
    responses

4. _____

past history
learning sets
physiological state
species and
    genetic
    differences

OTHER FACTORS

In a brief treatment, there is no possibility of citing the many specific variables which could, in any given instance, influence the rate of conditioning. There are two other factors to which recognition will be given because of their oft-noted influence.

Training variables such as overlearning and distributed practice have been shown to affect either acquisition or resistance to extinction or both. In the case of *overlearning,* the effects are shown in greater resistance to extinction of the habit which is well practiced or in the rate of learning a new task after overlearning another. Overlearning, then, may improve *retention* of a habit and may retard or facilitate the learning of a new habit depending upon, among other factors, the similarity of the new task to the old, The last point falls under the heading of *transfer of training.* Transfer of training is *positive* when overlearning a task facilitates the learning of a new task, and *negative* when it interferes with the learning of a new task.

Distributed practice refers to the schedule of training trials and is usually dichotomized as *massed practice* versus *spaced practice.* As implied, *massed trials* refers to a large number of trials per unit of time, for example, twenty trials per hour on two separate hours each day, while *spaced trials* refers to trials with an extended temporal interval between them, such as rest periods ranging from five minutes to a day or more between trials. The effects of distributed practice on acquisition and on extinction are complex, and generalizations are risky. Massed practice has been shown to increase resistance to extinction under some conditions and to decrease resistance to extinction under others. Massing of practice trials frequently retards acquisition, particularly when the massing is heavy, that is, when the intertrial interval is very brief and a large number of trials is given each day. Apparently, when trials are massed, an inhibition of effort or reactive inhibition occurs. When the trials are properly spaced, the inhibition generated by responding is dissipated with rest. Too long an intertrial interval may retard conditioning since there is an opportunity for forgetting to occur (where *forgetting* refers most often to interference with the learning of subsequent events rather than to nonuse of the habit).

Overlearning has been shown to improve retention of a habit. If, after subjects A and B have acquired a specific terminal behavior, fourteen additional training trials are provided for A, and forty additional training trials are provided for B, which subject will exhibit the greater amount of overlearning? _____ Which subject should retain the habit longer? _____

subject B

subject B

○ Overlearning facilitates learning when the tasks to be learned are (similar, dissimilar).

similar

○ When two tasks contain some elements which are similar and some which are dissimilar, the learning of one task may (facilitate, interfere with) the learning of the other.

interfere with

○ *Transfer of training* is positive when the tasks are very _____, and _____ when learning one task interferes with learning a second task.

similar
negative

The rate of learning may depend also on whether the training trials are massed or spaced. A large number of trials in an hour would be an example of (massed, spaced) practice.

massed

If a twenty-minute rest period were given after each trial, we would consider this schedule to be _____ practice.

spaced

The effects of distributed practice on learning are not entirely consistent. However, some spacing of practice, assuming that the interval of time is not too great, tends to increase the rate of learning, while the _____ of practice tends to retard learning.

massing

positive

massed
spaced
spaced

○ Complete the following:

1. Transfer of training is _____ when overlearning a task facilitates the learning of a new task.

2. Two schedules of training trials under distributed practice are _____ and _____.

3. A form of _____ practice is usually most effective during conditioning.

Instrumental Learning

and Classical Conditioning Compared

Many of the similarities and differences between instrumental learning and classical conditioning have been pointed out in previous sections; therefore, only the highlights will be noted here for the purpose of bringing the nature of the respective models to a focus.

One fundamental question to be considered is, *Are these two forms of learning or only two labels for the same essential process?* When one focuses on the models for training, there are clearly two forms, the nature of which have been considered thoroughly earlier in the book; thus, no one seriously proposes that the training procedures are the same. If one focuses on the learning processes, the similarities between the models are far greater than the differences. In each case, we have discussed stimulus and response generalization, stimulus discrimination, secondary reinforcement (higher-order conditioning), extinction, inhibition, etc.; it is evident that a common core of terms can be used for both models. It is also clear that these variables tend to produce the same essential effects on both models.

Still, there is a persisting belief that the two forms are not necessarily models of the same behavior. The question is difficult to answer at this stage of our knowledge. It appears to be impossible to conduct a pure study of either classical conditioning or instrumental learning. The work of Solomon (1964) and his students (LoLordo and Rescorla, 1964; Overmier, 1964) shows clearly that Pavlovian contingencies are usually present in instrumental training, and Sheffield has observed that "the important derivation is that every instrumental situation is a classical conditioning situation, with reward as US and response-produced cues as CS" (1965, p. 317). Further, unless the *same response* is conditioned by the separate training procedures, comparisons between the models are risky; yet, relatively few responses have been found which can be conditioned by both methods.

The inclination is to agree with Mowrer (1960) that there are two learning processes under consideration, rather than one. In the case of classical conditioning, the process is associated with involuntary responses, particularly emotional responses. Classical conditioning of these reponses tends to result in qualitatively better habit formation than does instrumental training. Reinforcement in the sense of rewards and punishments is not a critical variable in classical conditioning of involuntary responses, particularly when these responses are of a type which produce little, if any, sensory feedback. Temporal contiguity between the conditioned stimulus and the unconditioned stimulus is of critical importance.

In operant learning, the process is associated with voluntary responses, and Thorndike's "law of effect" is applicable. Rewards and punishments can be shown to strengthen those responses which produce sufficient feedback to signal to the organism that it has responded, and make it possible for the organism to associate its response with the S^r (Sheffield, 1965). If this position is valid, then only those involuntary responses which meet this condition should be conditionable with either method. The problem is to find an involuntary response which provides sensory feedback; then to design an instrumental-training study in which the effects of the Pavlovian contingencies can be separated from those of the instrumental training; and then to design a classical conditioning study without an instrumental component or in which the effects of the instrumental component can be separated from the effects of the classical conditioning model. This problem is posed to indicate the difficulties confronted by learning theorists in devising critical studies of differing theoretical positions on the same phenomena.

Reinforcement and Punishment in the Control

of HumanBehavior by Social Agencies

6

C. B. Ferster worked with B. F. Skinner from 1950 to 1955; from 1957 to 1963 he was engaged in research on operant learning at the Institute for Psychiatric Research with a joint appointment at the University of Indiana. This article is concerned with a program for the instrumental training of psychiatric patients by manipulating parts of the patients' environment. The paper is included in this volume as (1) a review of the major concepts of operant learning and (2) an extension of these concepts to persistent and complex social problems.

Clinical psychiatry and psychology depend on fundamental experimental analyses of behavior just as other fields of medicine depend on the basic sciences of physiology, biochemistry, and pharmacology. The slow development of basic natural-scientific analyses of behavior has resulted in clinical practices developed by rule of thumb or in terms of special theories unrelated to a fundamental or systematic behavioral analysis.

Ferster, C. B., in *Psychiat. Res. Reps.*, 1958, 10, 101–118. Reprinted with the permission of the author and the publisher from the article of the same title.

Behavioral experimentation with animals has been a continuous, although small contribution, to clinical theory and practice. The work of Pavlov on the conditioned reflex has provided the main source for much of the extensions to clinical problems. John B. Watson and his students first applied the conditioned reflex to the experimental development, elimination, and generalization of phobic reactions in children.[8] Later, N. E. Miller, S. Dollard, and O. H. Mowrer and others extended the conditioned reflex to a wider range of human performances and clinical problems.[2,5,6] The work of B. F. Skinner has given further impetus to applications to problems of psychiatric rehabilitation and therapy by an experimental analysis of "operant" behavior: the behavior of organisms which exists because of its effect on the environment in contrast with the reflex behavior analyzed by Pavlov.[1,7] Using the framework of Skinner's theoretical and experimental analysis, this paper outlines a program to change the behavior of psychiatric patients or generate new behavior by manipulating the actual environmental events maintaining a performance. The manipulatable events in the present and past environment of an organism are used to analyze the current performance in terms of the general processes already dealt with experimentally in animals and humans. The role of positive reinforcement and its corollaries in determining behavior is emphasized over aversive control.

THE NATURE OF THE SOCIAL AGENCY

Most of the behavior of organisms exists because of its effect on the environment (operant reinforcement). The paradigm is: An event following a given instance of behavior subsequently increases the frequency of occurrence of that behavior. The verbal response "Good morning" is maintained because it produces a reply from most audiences. In the absence of a reply, the response would disappear. Not all events have this property, and those that do are called reinforcements. Most human behavior is social because it has its effect on other organisms, which in turn arrange the reinforcements; this is in contrast to the physical environment, which reinforces directly. The same reinforcement paradigm may be extended to larger groups of people, such as social institutions and agencies; less well-defined groups involved in social practices, codes of conduct, etc.; small groups, such as the milieu in a certain factory, or neighborhood "gang" of children. These social practices ultimately refer to a set of reinforcements and punishments which the people who constitute the social agency or social practice apply to the behavior of an individual. The social situation is unique only in so far as other organisms mediate the reinforcements, punishments, or other important environmental effects.

A fundamental psychological analysis must deal with the behavior of the individual, and the functional dimensions of social behavior appear only when they are expressed in terms of the consequences that the members of a group of people arrange for an individual. Social approval, for example, refers to a high disposition to supply favorable consequences to a wide range of specific behaviors of the individual; and conversely, a low disposition to arrange punishments. Similarly, an individual with "social prestige" is one whose repertoire is reinforcing to members of a group, and will maintain the behavior of listening, reading, seeking close contact, and supplying reinforcements designed to maximize further performances.

Other social institutions such as law, government, religious agencies, and the family arrange very specific consequences which are somewhat easier to specify. The law and government, for example, have effects on the individual, largely by punishing specified forms of behavior by fines and incarceration. The religious agencies have some of their effects on the behaviors of the individual by similar processes. The punishments of hell and the rewards of heaven, as well as the more usual contingencies involved in the approval and disapproval by the membership of the religious agency, are used to maintain or suppress various behaviors.

THE LARGE ORDER OF MAGNITUDE OF SOCIAL CONTROL

The importance of social behavior in human affairs is heightened by the fact that the majority of human reinforcements are mediated by another individual. Many of the reinforcements deriving their effect from groups of people have a larger order of magnitude of effect than reinforcements supplied only by a single individual or the physical environment. The heightened control by social reinforcement comes about because:

1. Some reinforcements are possible only when a performance is carried out in connection with other individuals. The appeal of the parade and uniform comes primarily from the prestige which the individual can share only by being a member of a group which in turn is important to the community. The process referred to here is similar to

identification in dynamic psychology. Other examples in which the individual can have an effect in the community only when he behaves in concert with other individuals include the "gang," the revival meeting, and the cooperative action of three men lifting an object too heavy for any one of them.

2. Large numbers of individuals can potentially arrange reinforcements and punishments contingent on the behavior of the individual. The potential of an audience in rewarding or punishing depends in turn on the relevance of the reinforcements and punishments for the behavioral repertoire of the individual. The larger the number of individuals who can potentially reward, punish, or discontinue reinforcing behavior, the greater the effect is likely to be. Also, as the social agency involves more persons, there is less chance that an individual can avoid the punishment by escaping to another social group or to another environment for the reinforcements to maintain his existing repertoire. The control on the speaker by a relevant and effective audience illustrates this property of social reinforcements. When the audience has only a few members, the speaker may react to punishment or nonreinforcement by turning to other audiences. As the size of the audience increases, however, the effect of the contingencies they arrange on the behavior of the speaker becomes more and more inevitable. The control achieved in brain washing illustrates the large order of magnitude of effect from controlling all of the audiences affecting an individual. Similarly, a group practice or a set of cultural mores has a large order of magnitude of contol because the larger number of individuals who will arrange the reinforcements and punishments which constitute the social practice make this almost inevitable.

CHARACTERIZATION OF THE BEHAVIOR OF THE PSYCHIATRIC PATIENT IN TERMS OF A FUNCTIONAL ANALYSIS

Many psychiatric patients or potentially psychiatric patients may be characterized as having repertoires whose performances are not producing the reinforcements of the world: because too much behavior is being punished; because nearly all of the individual's behavior is maintained by avoiding aversive consequences rather than producing positive effects; or a combination of all of these. A potential reinforcing environment exists for every individual, however, if he will only emit the required performances on the proper occasions. One has merely to paint the picture, write the symphony, produce the machine, tell the funny story, give affection artfully, and the world will respond in kind with prestige, money, social response, and love. Conversely, a repertoire which will make contact with the reinforcements of the world will be subsequently maintained because of the effect of the reinforcement on the performance. The problem is social because most of the reinforcements are mediated by other individuals.

A deficient behavioral repertoire may arise because:

Inadequate reinforcement history

Under this category belong individuals who are not making contact with important parts of their environment simply because their history did not include a set of experiences (educational) which could develop these performances during the normal maturation of the individual. Especially in the area of everyday social contacts, considerable skill is necessary for producing social reinforcements, and the absence of this skill either results in an individual without a social repertoire or one who achieves affects on his social environment by indirect means, as, for example, using aversive stimulation to gain attention. It is possible that this latter behavior would disappear if the individual had a repertoire which would be effective in producing positive reinforcements. The existence of weak, positively reinforced repertoires, particularly in the field of ordinary social contacts, could result in "unsocial behavior" designed to affect the behavior of others by generating aversive conditions which are strong enough to produce avoidance, escape, and punishment. The reinforcing effect of these "anti-social" reactions might be large only in respect to the weak, positively reinforced repertoire.

Schedule of reinforcement

The schedule of reinforcement of a given performance might also produce a weakened disposition to engage in this performance so that the normal reinforcements do not occur. This kind of absence of behavior would be produced particularly in situations where large amounts of work are required for reinforcements, as, for example, in the case of the writer, housewife, student, or salesman, where reinforcement depends on a fixed amount of work. The individual's repertoire contains the required performances, but the existing schedule of reinforcement is such as to weaken the repertoire and thereby prevent its occurrence even though the correct form of the behavior would be available if the schedules of reinforcement were more optimal.

Punishment may distort a performance which otherwise would be reinforced

The absence of adequate repertoires in the individual could result from the distortion of the form of the behavior so that the performance does not have its customary effect. Excessive punishment may also generate avoidance behavior which is strong enough to be prepotent over the currently positively reinforced repertoires of the individual.

TECHNIQUES AVAILABLE TO THE THERAPIST

The basic principles governing the development and maintenance of behavior are relevant to the task of generating new performances in an individual whose existing repertoire is not making contact with the reinforcements potentially available to him. The same principles are also relevant to the problem of generating adequate repertoires which will escape punishment.

Some of the reasons for a currently inadequate behavioral repertoire may be found in the history of the organism, perhaps even in the early infancy. In many cases, however, the behavioral history of an individual is inaccessible. To the extent, however, that a current environment exists which can potentially maintain performances in all of the important segments in the individual's life by positive reinforcement, the history of the individual is relevant only in so far as it is useful in assessing the current repertoire of the individual. A functional program of therapy relying on the manipulatable factors in the patient's environment may have important therapeutic effects, without reference to speculative accounts of the patient's history, the current verbal reports of his feelings, and attitudes. Little more is to be desired if a patient is content with his lot, works productively in a job, achieves affection and respect from his fellows, has an adequate sexual and home life, enjoys food and drink in moderation, and has diversions and adequate social relations.

If the therapist is ultimately to be successful, he must alter the relationship between the patient's performance in a wide variety of social situations and the reinforcement and punishment which will result. The therapist initially has the prestige of his profession and social position and the potential reinforcing effect involved in transference. These properties of the therapist, initially at least, give him the ability to change the patient's performance in at least some situations outside of the room in which the therapy is conducted. Ultimately, the reinforcement of these performances in the patient's environment will maintain the continued attention of the patient to the therapist's advice.

THE PROCESSES BY WHICH SOCIAL AGENCIES AFFECT THE BEHAVIOR OF THE INDIVIDUAL

The major processes of behavior provide the technology for generating and eliminating behavior in the individual and are basic to the analysis of social effects. In the final analysis, the agency can have an effect on the individual only by arranging some environmental event contingent on the behavior of the individual. The social situation differs from the nonsocial one by the mediation of another organism in the delivery of the reward, punishment, or other consequence. It must be assumed, in the absence of contrary evidence, that the processes and laws operating in social situations are the same ones which are the basis for all behavioral processes.

Reinforcement

Reinforcement is the most important process by which behavior is generated and maintained. Most of an organism's behavior exists because of the effect on the environment, perhaps with the exception of the psychotic whose repertoire reflects the absence of behavior maintained with positive reinforcement. Reinforcement differs from the colloquial reward in its specificity; it is the immediate environmental consequences of a specific performance. The major effect of reinforcement needs to be distinguished from the classical or Pavlovian-type conditioning where the conditioned response is some elicited reflex, usually autonomic. The increase in the frequency of occurrence of the performance that is reinforced is the property of reinforcement that permits the tremendous variety and subtlety that occurs in the field of "voluntary" behavior as opposed to reflex and autonomic behavior.

Most reinforcements of everyday life are social rather than involving immediately important biological conditions. These social-maintaining-events operate as reinforcements because they are in a chain of events leading ultimately to a more basic consequence. Money provides an example of a conditioned reinforcer—*par excellence*—which derives its effect because its possession is a condition under which other performances will produce basic environmental effects. The important social consequences of money occur because the reinforcing properties of money nearly always depend immediately or ultimately upon the behavior of other individuals. Similarly, a smile can reinforce behavior because an individual who is smiling is more likely to supply subsequent reinforcements than one who is not.

As with money, many reinforcements in human behavior can be effective in the absence of any specific deprivation, unlike most reinforcements demonstrated in animal experiments. These "generalized" reinforcements maintain much of human behavior, and have large order of magnitudes of effect because their reinforcing power comes from a variety of reinforcements and deprivations and does not depend upon a current level of deprivation. This is especially true of nearly all reinforcements mediated by other organisms, because the mediation by another organism, in general, permits the application of a wider range of reinforcements. Other examples of generalized reinforcers include paying attention, affection, saying "right," or "correct," smiling, etc. These are important reinforcements because they are the usual conditions under which another organism will reinforce a behavior of an individual.

The development of complex forms of behavior: "shaping"

A major corollary of reinforcement is a procedure by which a reinforcing agency can produce progressively complex forms of behavior by small increments from a preceding simpler form. A commonly used animal-demonstration experiment illustrates the process. If we wish to teach a pigeon to peck at a small disc on the wall of his chamber, we first establish a reinforcer by presenting grain to the bird whenever the grain hopper is illuminated. The bird soon comes to approach the hopper only when it is illuminated, and it is then possible to use the lighted hopper as a reinforcement. The bird faces in the direction of the small disc, is reinforced, and the effect is an immediate increase in the tendency to face the disc. Reinforcement is then withheld until the bird nods slightly in the direction of the disc, and the reinforcement of this slightly more complex form increases its frequency. When the bird is nodding in the direction of the disc, the variation in the magnitude of the nod is noted and the reinforcement is shifted in the direction of those nods bringing the bird's head closer to the disc. By continuing the process, the pigeon can soon be made to strike the disc.

The same process occurs in the development of human behavior, particularly in the formative years. The process by which complex forms are generated is relevant to the therapy situation whenever a patient is lacking parts of the complex repertoire necessary to achieve reinforcement from the complicated social environment. Simply telling a patient what kind of performance is necessary for reinforcement will seldom generate the required complex performance. The situation is analogous to the golfer who would like to drive the ball 250 yards. The necessary performance must be acquired in small steps, beginning with an existing repertoire and approximating the final performance with intermediate, temporary reinforcements.

The therapist is in a position to "shape" behavior in a patient by beginning with a performance already in his repertoire and exposing him to selected portions of his environment designed to generate the new, more complex form. The therapist can select an environment accessible to the patient in which a reinforcing agent is operating which will reinforce with a high degree of probability a variation in the patient's performance in the direction of the desired, more complicated form.

For example, consider the hypothetical case of an individual who has never acquired the performances necessary for facile enough social contact. The patient's current repertoire contains enough verbal behavior to permit him to talk to the therapist. A first step in this hypothetical case might be to send the patient to a college campus one morning and have him say "Good morning" to several people he passes. The environment of the campus is chosen to almost guarantee the reinforcement of this response. This kind of exercise would also illustrate to the patient general verbal processes in human behavior where it is possible to command a verbal response from an audience. In a similar vein, the complexity of the verbal repertoire of the individual could be increased further. Commands, such as "Could you please tell me the time," also produce almost inevitable responses in most situations; and if the rate of development of the new behavior is made small enough from the preceding forms which the patient is emitting successfully, there would be no difficulty from nonreinforcement because of inaudible remarks, mumbling, or other distortion of the behavior which would prevent the reinforcement.

Group therapy or psychodrama could also be adapted to the task of generating new performances as an intermediate step to be used between "office therapy" and exercises using outside environments accessible to the patient. Patients could use each other, under the direction of a therapist, to develop skills necessary in normal social practice. The therapist would set tasks for each patient carefully graded so as to be within the range of the existing behavioral repertoire. Groups of patients would provide an environment potentially capable of supporting at least some kinds of performances, and the exercises would be designed to take advantage of these reinforcements which are possible within the hospital environment. Exercises could be designed, for example, to illustrate and develop behavior which makes it possible to command behavior from another individual: the effect of saying "please," kinds of performances which will engender conversation, cooperation in projects, techniques for achieving nonsocial reinforcements as in reading, and developing productive skills as in occupational therapy. Many of these goals are already present in many hospital situations. What is required is a program of administration which will maintain motivation during the development of the complex repertoire and establish the behavior firmly enough to provide a basis to go on to a next, more complex form.

Another example on a slightly more complex level might be the behavior of a shy boy or girl having difficulty in social and sexual relations with the opposite sex. The first task is to specify the necessary performances for achieving the potential social reinforcements. A practical program requires the development of a repertoire capable of getting a date and carrying it through adequately. The practical program would include the development of auxiliary skills such as dancing, skating, card-playing, and various sports which would provide performances predominately nonsocial which could be carried out in the company of the opposite sex and provide opportunities for the reinforcements of other kinds of behavior. As in the previous example, it would be necessary to begin with the existing repertoire and develop a situation in which the audience composed of the opposite sex can reinforce the appropriate behavior whenever it occurs. The situation is a potentially difficult one because any nonreinforcement will have large effects on an initially weak verbal repertoire. A series of exercises could be constructed beginning, for example, with a situation in which little is required verbally, such as playing cards, and the emission of only those responses whose reinforcements are guaranteed, such as a command, reading, trite sayings, etc. The development of a repertoire leading to sexual activity would begin with performances designed to extend physical contact; for example, shaking hands, help over minor obstacles, congratulatory pat on the shoulder, etc.

To the extent that enough major performances in enough important areas can be generated, the fundamental historical reason behind the original disinclination to associate with the opposite sex, or avoid contact with the opposite sex, is no longer essential to the correction of the situation. So long as the individual is spending the time with the opposite sex, enjoying adequate sexuo-social relations, and engaged in normal social give-and-take, the historical factors are no longer relevant.

Intermittent reinforcement

Social reinforcements are intermittent because the reinforcements mediated by another organism are less reliable than those produced by the physical environment. This arises because the social reinforcement depends upon behavioral processes in the reinforcer which are not always under good control by the reinforcee. For example, if one is asked to look outside and report whether it is raining, many factors in the repertoire of the listener could interfere with the successful completion of the report: the listener is afraid of height, some more urgent audience catches the attention of the listener, the listener happened not to be attentive at the moment the request is made, the listener's eye glasses are off at the moment, etc. In contrast, the effects of most behavior on the physical environment is almost inevitable.

The nature of the intermittency has a great influence on the disposition to engage in a given behavior. It is possible to produce an almost complete cessation of some behavior which the individual has emitted literally thousands of times by alteration of the schedule of reinforcement. Similarly, identical frequencies of reinforcements on different reinforcement schedules produce widely differing dispositions to engage in the behavior.

The history by which the individual is exposed to many schedules is also of great importance. Certain schedules of reinforcement will sustain behavior normally if approached in gradual steps but will produce complete cessation (abulia) if the individual is exposed to the final schedule at once. In the most prevalent schedule of reinforcement found in human affairs (ratio reinforcement), the reinforcement occurs as a function of a certain number of instances of a performance. One of the major properties of this schedule of reinforcement is a decline in the disposition to emit the behavior when the amount of work for reinforcement becomes too large. This lessened disposition occurs particularly as inability to begin work just after a reinforcement. The disinclination of the novelist to begin a new novel just after completing one is a pure example of this effect. There is some suggestion that there are inductive effects among the various repertoires of the individual.

An optimal schedule of reinforcement in one area will help sustain a performance under a less optimal schedule of reinforcement in another area; and, conversely, reinforcement on unoptimal schedules of reinforcement may have the opposite effect of weakening a repertoire whose reinforcement schedule is more optimal. These "ratio" or piecework schedules of reinforcement are contrasted with another major schedule class where the reinforcement of a response becomes more likely with passage of time since the previous reinforcement. These schedules are less prevalent in human affairs than ratio schedules, and tend to produce a level of performance more appropriate to the frequency of reinforcement regardless of the history of the individual. Examples of this latter class of schedules of reinforcement include looking in the mailbox when the mail delivery occurs somewhat unpredictably (variable-interval reinforcement), and looking into the pot on the stove as the water is being boiled.

Optimum parameters of a schedule of reinforcement may also result in very large amounts of behavior and a strong disposition to engage in the reinforced behavior. The behavior of the gambler is an excellent example where an explicit program of reinforcement (technically classified variable-ratio) generates a strong disposition to gamble, even though the individual operates at a loss over a longer period of time. Here the heightened disposition to gamble arising from the optimal variable-ratio schedule of reinforcements (even the loser wins frequently) overrides the over-all low net reinforcement.

Applications to therapy　To the extent that a patient's difficulties result from inadequate or unoptimal reinforcement of important repertories, there is little in the immediate therapy situation which can change his performance. The salesman, for example, whose ratio of "selling" to sales becomes too high and suffers from irritability, moodiness, and the disinclination to work, needs more sales for "less selling" before his situation can improve. Arthur Miller's play "Death of a Salesman" provides an excellent example of the deterioration in a performance that can come about under a "piecework" schedule of reinforcement.

It is possible that the general condition of an individual whose behavior is weak because of too much behavior emitted with too little reinforcement resembles conditions arising from aversive control. This may be especially true when the "strained" repertoire is supplemented by aversive conditions such as threats which can be avoided only by emitting more of the "strained" behavior. For example, the factory worker on a piecework pay schedule may be threatened, lose his job, or be fined when he stops working even though his rate of pay is proportional to the amount of work he does. Secondary factors may also influence the way in which a given repertoire is maintained on a schedule of reinforcement. Physical exhaustion, poor health, and inductive effects from other repertoires may produce strain under a schedule of reinforcement which under other conditions might have been satisfactory.

Early exposure to intermittent reinforcement Many behavioral repertoires are weak because of an accidental history which supplied an inadequate reinforcement at an early stage. This could come about especially when punishment produces forms of behavior which go unreinforced because they are distorted. An optimal schedule of reinforcement of a repertoire is essential at an early stage of development if a strong disposition to engage in the performance is to be maintained later under less optimal schedules. The genesis of avid gamblers illustrates the importance of the schedule of reinforcement during the initial acquisition of the repertoire. Professional gamblers, for example, will arrange a high frequency of reinforcement for the beginner in order to provide conditions under which the beginner will continue to gamble later when the schedule of reinforcement is less adequate. Similarly, at least a part of the difference between the person who continues to gamble, and those who failed to continue after a brief exposure, lies in the initial "luck." The fisherman is on the same schedule of reinforcement as the gambler, and the result is the same. The avid interest of the fishing devotee is extreme compared with others and probably represents the result of an optimal schedule of reinforcement during the initial fishing experiences.

The community maximizes the frequency of reinforcement during the educational phase of an individual by providing reinforcements for rough approximations to the ultimately effective forms. For example, a young child emitting the response "wawer" is likely to be reinforced by a glass of water, while the same response at a later stage of development will be unreinforced, or even punished. Thus, in the early stages of development of the repertoire a higher frequency of reinforcement is more easily achieved than later, when the community demands a more differentiated and closely specified form of behavior and environmental control. Whether newly developing behavior will persist depends upon whether the initial frequency and manner of reinforcement will sustain the performance as it comes under the control of the relevant stimuli, as the form of the behavior becomes more and more differentiated, and as the audience selectively reinforces more effective forms. Whenever a repertoire becomes weakened because of accidental nonreinforcement during the early development of the repertoire it becomes more difficult to reinstate the repertoire because the form of the behavior must now be more exact and under more precise environmental control than during the early stages of development.

Compare, for example, the successful and unsuccessful adult in his sexuo-social relations with the opposite sex. Very highly differentiated behavior under close stimulus control is required. Once an individual matures beyond a given age without developing the performances in respect to the opposite sex which will be reinforced, it becomes more difficult to acquire effective performances. The situation is comparable to the difficulties of the algebra student who tries to learn factoring without being facile in algebraic multiplication and division.

In cases where the individual's repertoire is inadequate because of an unoptimal schedule of reinforcement, it should be possible to do therapy by directing the individual to situations where some approximation to the effective form of the behavior will be reinforced. Only after the repertoire is acquired in a form that is maximally effective in achieving reinforcement, would the individual be directed into situations where progressively more nonreinforcement could occur.

Superstitious reinforcement

A reinforcing event will increase the disposition to engage in the behavior reinforced even though the reinforcement is spurious or accidental. As in the case of the gambler, the chance history of reinforcement is important in determining whether accidental or spurious reinforcements will sustain the behavior. Once there is some tendency to emit the behavior as the result of some accidental reinforcements, the resulting tendency to continue behaving increases the likelihood that the behavior will be in progress subsequently when another reinforcement occurs. These superstitious performances are most likely to occur under high motivation, as for example the gambler addressing the dice "come seven" or the "posturing" of the bowler. These spurious reinforcements are probably even more effective in the field of aversive control. If the aversively maintained behavior is conditioned strongly enough, the behavior may never extinguish because the avoidance behavior prevents the occurrence of the conditioned aversive stimuli which now would no longer be followed by the aversive event.

Here again the therapist is in a position to select special situations in the patient's environment where the positive reinforcement occurs even though the superstitious behavior is withheld; or in those cases where the superstition is maintained by "avoiding" an aversive event, the behavior is withheld in a situation where the primary aversive event will not occur. Some preliminary experiments in the latter case by English workers have shown large effectiveness of this manner of therapy in dealing with phobic behavior in selected individuals.[1]

Stimulus control of behavior

The reinforcement or punishment of a verbal or nonverbal response depends upon the nature of the audience. Not all performances of an individual are reinforced on all occasions, and the situation characteristically present when a given kind of behavior is reinforced comes to control the likelihood that the performance will occur. Nearly all of the behavior of the normal adult comes under very close stimulus control of the various audiences to which he is exposed. Details of speech as subtle as vocabulary and intonation change with different audiences. The thematic material of a conversation varies widely depending upon the audience, from shop talk to a co-worker to the "baby-talk" maximally effective in producing a reaction from an infant. Poor development of stimulus control will result in a lower net frequency of reinforcement. The nonreinforcement of behavior that occurs during the development of stimulus control is tantamount to intermittent reinforcement until the stimulus control develops. To the extent that performances are reinforced only on specific occasions and by particular audiences, a failure of stimulus control results in an increase in the proportion of an individual's behavior which goes unreinforced.

The normal maturation of an individual into childhood and adulthood illustrates the interrelation between intermittent reinforcement and stimulus control. We reinforce almost any form of behavior in infants and very young children so long as there is a remote resemblance to the required performance. As the child grows older, however, the reinforcement is continually shifted in the direction of forms which approximate the normal cultural practices. Many members of the community will reinforce the behavior of the young child even though it has little importance for the listener. As the child develops through school-age, however, the audience becomes more selective and now properly differentiated forms of behavior will go unreinforced if they are not reinforcing for the listener. Hence, a further possibility of nonreinforcement arises whenever a performance is inappropriate for a given audience. The better an individual's performances are controlled by the environment, therefore, the more optimal will be the schedule of positive reinforcement. Inadequate stimulus and audience control of behavior could be one of the conditions under which an inadequate repertoire would develop because of performances occurring where they will not be reinforced and not occurring when they will be reinforced.

Just as accidental reinforcements may generate forms of behavior which are superstitious in the sense that the behavior is not a necessary condition for the occurrence of the reinforcement, it is possible for irrelevant aspects of a situation to acquire stimulus control of a performance. Every occasion on which a reinforcement occurs has multiple dimensions, and the aspects which come to control are somewhat undetermined until there are differential consequences in terms of the various elements. For example, an individual has a history in which many of the people who have given good advice have worn double-breasted suits, bow-ties, and spoken with a cosmopolitan accent. There will, therefore, be a heightened disposition to follow advice from persons exhibiting these characteristics until enough individuals have been encountered who shared some of these properties but have given bad advice. In a similar manner, an audience resembling a parent may increase the likelihood of occurrence of performances previously reinforced by a parent, even though that audience is not a potential reinforcer. This kind of inadequate stimulus control may simply be an accident of the historical conditions under which past reinforcements have occurred in situations which have multiple dimensions, some of which are irrelevant. More adequate stimulus control can develop only by exposure to the irrelevant aspect of the situation and the corresponding nonreinforcement.

General motivational factors may also heighten the control by irrelevant aspects of a situation or audience. The man lost on the desert without water is more likely to mistake irrelevant stimuli for water.

It should be possible to sharpen the stimulus control of behavior by alternately exposing the individual to situations containing the various elements separately and allowing the resulting reinforcement and non-reinforcement to strengthen the tendency to emit the performance on the relevant occasions and weaken the disposition to emit the behavior when the irrelevant aspects are present.

It may be possible to design exercises using the principles governing the development of stimulus control of behavior to increase the sharpness of the stimulus control of a patient's behavior. What is required is to teach the patient to attend to the differential effects his performances have on the environment. The earlier example of the patient learning to say "Good morning" provides an example of the type of exercise that may be possible. After the patient is saying "Good morning" successfully in situations where the reinforcement is all but inevitable, the therapist points up situations where the likelihood of a verbal response of this kind being reinforced is near zero and explains the relevant factors responsible. For example, the patient is instructed to say "Good morning" to a man running to catch a train or to workers entering a factory a few minutes after the official starting time. Further exercises would include alternating between the situations where "Good morning" will be reinforced and those in which "Good morning" will go unreinforced. The complexity of the exercises could be gradually increased as more and more complex forms were available as a result of the "shaping" from the earlier exercises. Eventually exercises would be carried out in which the thematic material of a conversation would be manipulated in respect to the interest of the audience.

Aversive control

In social situations most control by aversive stimuli involves the removal or discontinuation of positive reinforcement rather than some kind of primary aversive stimulation. The usual social punishments are (1) *disapproval:* a state of affairs where the reinforcer is not likely to continue reinforcements for specific performances; (2) *fines:* a loss of money or privilege effectively reduces the amount of various kinds of behavior that can be reinforced; (3) *criticism:* an indication of specific performances which will not be reinforced, or which will bring about nonreinforcement in other spheres, and (4) *incarceration:* the extreme case where large portions of the repertoire of the individual can no longer produce their characteristic reinforcement.

While the discontinuation of positive reinforcement can be used as a punishment, it is important to distinguish between the effect of non-reinforcement *per se* and its use as a punishment. As noted earlier, the nonreinforcement of a performance on one occasion and its consistent reinforcement on a second occasion is the main process by which environmental control of behavior takes place. The decline of frequency of occurrence of a performance as a function of nonreinforcement has very different properties from punishment by the discontinuation of reinforcement. In the latter case, the punishment is carried out by presenting a stimulus which is already correlated with a low probability of response because of previous nonreinforcement. Its aversive effect probably derives from the over-all importance in the repertoire of the individual of the behavior being blocked. The simple discontinuation of positive reinforcement shares some of the properties of an aversive stimulus, particularly during the transient phase while the frequency of the nonreinforced performance is still falling. Once the stimulus control is established, however, the resulting low disposition to engage in the extinguished behavior allows concurrent repertoires to take over. The salient feature of punishment is that an aversive stimulus is applied to some performance which is maintained by a positive reinforcement; thus the original source of strength of the performance is still present and the performance can reappear in some strength when the punishment is discontinued. This is to be contrasted with simple extinction or nonreinforcement where the maintaining event for the behavior is discontinued and the performance no longer occurs simply because it no longer has its characteristic effect on the environment.

A second major effect of an aversive stimulus is the disruption of substantial segments of the repertoire of the individual by the situation characteristically preceding the aversive event. The pre-aversive situation (anxiety) has an emotional effect in the sense that it produces a state of affairs where there is a disruption of parts of the individual's repertoire not directly related to the aversive event. For example, the student just before the crucial examination, the patient in the dentist's waiting room, the child just before the parent discovers the broken ash tray, and the soldier just before the battle will all show considerable disruption of the normal repertoire; marked changes in the frequency of occurrence of all of the performances which might normally occur under these situations without the aversive event.

The third function of the aversive stimulus is in maintaining behavior because it terminates or postpones (escapes or avoids) the aversive event. The examples of these kinds of reinforcements in a normal repertoire include opening or closing a window to alter an extreme in temperature; buying fuel in advance of cold weather, or making an apology to reduce the threat of punishment.

The clinical effects of excess of punishment have been fairly widely recognized and analyzed, and much of current therapy is analyzed as eliminating the aversive effects of situations which no longer are associated with punishment.

The disruptive effects of aversive control will interfere with the development of the precise forms of behavior being generated by positive reinforcement. This would be particularly true in the area of social contact such as sexual behavior where punishment is widely applied, and where complex and precise forms of behavior are required. A practical program would be designed to develop forms of behavior which would avoid punishment as well as maximize reinforcement. Situations which would disrupt positively maintained repertoires because of a history of punishment would have to be approached in small steps so that the strength of the positively maintained behavior is large in respect to the disruptive effect and the aversive history.

Another corollary of aversive control is its prepotency over positively reinforced behavior. The use of aversive control generates immediate escape and avoidance behavior, and the wide use of punishment and aversive stimulation as a technique of control probably stems from the immediate effects which this kind of stimulation achieves as opposed to the slower development of behavior by a positive reinforcement. When an aversive condition is set up in order to generate some performance which must ultimately be maintained by positive reinforcement (for example, nagging), the control often backfires when the individual terminates the nagging by counter aversive control rather than emitting the performance which will reinforce the "nagger" and terminate the nagging. It is possible that some psychiatric patients have repertoires almost entirely composed of immediate reactions to threats and punishments which are entirely prepotent over positively reinforced repertoires. To the extent that this is true, the development of strong positively reinforced repertoires would provide an avenue of therapy.

SUMMARY

The present analysis of the psychiatric patient characterizes him in terms of the reinforcements immediately available in his environment, or potentially available if changes can be brought about in his repertoire. The general plan is to bring to bear toward the rehabilitation of the patient whatever techniques are available for generating new behavior and eliminating existing performances. Potential reinforcements for almost any kind of behavioral repertoire exist in some environment. By selectively directing the patient into currently accessible reinforcing environments, it may be possible to build almost any kind of repertoire by proceeding in small steps from a performance that is currently maintained in one part of the patient's environment to a slightly more complex performance which could be reinforced in another situation accessible to the patient. All the known principles by which behavior is generated, differentiated, brought under stimulus control, and eliminated would be used. The major processes appealed to were: (1) Reinforcement; those environmental events which produce an increase in the frequency of occurrence of a specific performance they follow. (2) Differentiation of complex forms; a major corollary of reinforcement which makes it possible to begin with a performance which is currently reinforced and then gradually increase the complexity of the performance by reinforcing progressively more complex forms. (3) The long-term maintenance of a performance by manipulating the occurrence of instances of nonreinforcement of the performance. (4) The stimulus control of behavior; deliberate nonreinforcement of the performance on one occasion coupled with reinforcement of that same performance on another occasion in order to sharpen the environmental or stimulus control of the performance. (5) Elimination of behavior by choosing an environment in which the behavior can occur without punishment or reinforcement, whichever is relevant.

It is possible that many of the symptoms which bring the patient to therapy are largely a by-product of inadequate positively reinforced repertoires; that the disposition to engage in the psychotic, neurotic, and pathological behaviors may seem strong when compared to weak existing repertoires but would disappear as soon as alternative effective ways of dealing with some accessible environment is generated.

The examples of exercises designed to generate positively reinforced repertoires and eliminate debilitating performances are intended only as suggestive. A satisfactory protocol for generating new performances can come about only from experience in an experimental program with patients carried out by persons with sufficient clinical skill.

The present analysis emphasizes the manipulatable aspects of environments potentially available to the patient. The behavior of the patient is treated directly as the subject matter of therapy rather than as a symptom of inner cause. Just as the current behavior of an individual developed as the result of the past exposure to some environment, the current repertoire should be amenable to a similar process in the current environment. To the extent that behavioral processes are reversible, it should be possible to change any performance by manipulating the relevant factor within the context of the same process in which it was originally generated.

References

1. **Ferster, C. B., and Skinner, B. F.** *Schedules of reinforcement.* New York: Appleton-Century-Crofts, 1957.
2. **Hull, C. L.** *Principles of behavior.* New York: Appleton-Century-Crofts, 1953.
3. **Lindsley, O. R.** Operant conditioning methods applied to research in chronic schizophrenia. *Psychiat. Res. Reps.,* 1956, **5,** 118–139.
4. **Meyer, V.** The treatment of two phobic patients on the basis of learning principles. *J. Abnorm. Soc. Psychol.,* 1953, **55,** 261–266.
5. **Miller, N. E., and Dollard, S.** *Personality and psychotherapy.* New York: McGraw-Hill, 1950.
6. **Mowrer, O. H.** A stimulus response analysis of anxiety and its role as a reinforcing agent. *Psychol. Rev.,* **46,** 553–566.
7. **Skinner, B. F.** *Science and human behavior.* New York: Macmillan, 1953.
8. **Watson, J. B., and Rayner, R.** Conditioned emotional reactions. *J. Exp. Psychol.,* **3,** 1–14.

Bibliography

Ban, T. A. *Conditioning and psychiatry*. Chicago: Aldine, 1964.

Bijou, S. W. Methodology for an experimental analysis of child behavior. *Psychol. Rep.*, 1957, **3**, 243–250.

Bijou, S. W. Operant or instrumental studies with children using baseline measures. Paper presented at a symposium, Recent Developments in Experimental Methods with Children, Amer. Psychol. Ass., Washington, 1958. Mimeographed.

Bitterman, M. E. The CS-US interval in classical and avoidance conditioning. In W. F. Prokasy (ed.), *Classical conditioning: A symposium*. New York: Appleton-Century-Crofts, 1965.

Blough, D. S. Experiments in animal psychophysics. *Sci. Amer.*, 1961, **205** (1), 113–123.

Brogden, W. J. Animal studies of learning. In Stevens, S. S. (ed.), *Handbook of experimental psychology*. New York: Wiley, 1951.

Candland, D. K., and Conklyn, D. H. Use of the "oddity problem" in teaching mentally retarded deaf-mutes to read: A pilot project. *Train. Sch. Bull.*, 1962, **59**, 38–41.

Cole, L. E. *Human behavior: Psychology as a bio-social science*. New York: World, 1953.

Cowles, J. T. Food-tokens as incentives for learning by chimpanzees. *Comp. Psychol. Monogr.,* 1937, **14** (71).

Deese, J. *The psychology of learning.* New York: McGraw-Hill, 1958.

Estes, W. K. The statistical approach to learning theory. In Koch, S. (ed.), *Psychology: A study of a science.* Vol. 2. New York: McGraw-Hill, 1959.

Eysenck, H. J. (ed.) *Behavior therapy and the neuroses.* New York: Pergamon, 1960.

Ferster, C. B. The use of the free operant in the analysis of behavior. *Psychol. Bull.,* 1953, **50,** 263–274.

Ferster, C. B. Reinforcement and punishment in the control of human behavior by social agencies. *Psychiat. Res. Rep.,* 1958, **10,** 101–118.

Griffard, C. D., and Peirce, J. T. Conditioned discrimination in the planarian. *Science,* 1964, **144,** 1472–1473.

Grossberg, J. M. Behavior therapy: A review. *Psychol. Bull.,* 1964, **62,** 73–88.

Group for the Advancement of Psychiatry. *Pavlovian conditioning and American psychiatry.* Symposium no. 9. New York: 1964.

Herrnstein, R. J. In defense of bird brains. *Atlantic Mon.,* 1965, **216** (3), 101–105.

Herrnstein, R. J., and Loveland, D. H. Complex visual concept in the pigeon. *Science,* 1964, **146,** 549–551.

Hilgard, E. R. Methods and procedures in the study of learning. In Stevens, S. S. (ed.), *Handbook of experimental psychology.* New York: Wiley, 1951.

Holland, J. G. Teaching machines: An application of principles from the laboratory. In *Proceedings of the 1959 Conference on Testing Problems.* Princeton: Educational Testing Service, 1959.

Holland, J. G., and Skinner, B. F. *The analysis of behavior.* New York: McGraw-Hill, 1961.

Homme, L. E., and Tosti, D. T. Contingency management and motivation. *NSPI J.,* 1965, **IV,** 14–16.

Hull, C. L. *Principles of behavior.* New York: Appleton-Century-Crofts, 1943.

Humphrey G. Extinction and negative adaptation. *Psychol. Rev.,* 1930, **37,** 361–363.

Hundt, A. G., and Premack, D. Running as both positive and negative reinforcer. *Science,* 1963, **142,** 1087–1088.

James, W. *The principles of psychology.* New York: Holt, 1890.

Kellogg, W. N. "Positive" and "negative" conditioning, without contraction of the essential muscles during the period of training. *Psychol. Bull.,* 1939, **36,** 575.

Kimble, G. A. *Hilgard and Marquis conditioning and learning.* New York: Appleton-Century-Crofts, 1961.

Kretch, D., and Crutchfield, R. S. *Theory and problems of social psychology.* New York: McGraw-Hill, 1948.

LoLordo, V. M., and Rescorla, R. A. Effects of a stimulus previously contrasted with shock upon ongoing avoidance responding. *Amer. Psychologist,* 1964, **19,** 520.

Lovibond, S. H. *Conditioning and enuresis.* New York: Pergamon, 1964.

Maier, N. R. F., and Schneirla, T. C. *Principles of animal psychology.* New York: McGraw-Hill, 1935.

Mowrer, O. H. Apparatus for the study and treatment of enuresis. *Amer. J. Psychol.,* 1938, **51,** 163–166.

Mowrer, O. H. *Learning theory and behavior.* New York: Wiley, 1960.

Overmier, J. B. Classical conditioning under curare with two US durations subsequently results in differential instrumental responding. *Amer. Psychologist,* 1964, **19,** 525.

Pavlov, I. P. *Conditioned reflexes* (translated by G. V. Anrep). London: Oxford, 1927.

Pavlov, I. P. *Lectures on conditioned reflexes* (translated by W. H. Gantt). New York: International Publishers, 1928.

Peckham, G. W., and Peckham, E. G. Some observations on the mental powers of spiders. *J. Morphol.,* 1887, **1,** 383–419.

Pennypacker, H. S. Measurement of the conditioned eyelid reflex. *Science,* 1964, **144,** 1248–1249.

Prokasy, W. F. *Classical conditioning: A symposium.* New York: Appleton-Century-Crofts, 1965.

Razran, G. The observable unconscious in current Soviet psychophysiology: Survey and interpretation of experiments in interoceptive conditioning. In L. E. Abt & B. F. Riess (eds.), *Progress in clinical psychology.* New York: Grune & Stratton, 1960.

Razran, G. The observable unconscious and the inferable conscious in current Soviet psychophysiology: Interoceptive conditioning, semantic conditioning, and the orienting reflex. *Psychol. Rev.,* 1961, **68,** 81–147.

Sheffield, F. D. Relation between classical conditioning and instrumental learning. In W. F. Prokasy (ed.), *Classical conditioning: A symposium.* New York: Appleton-Century-Crofts, 1965.

Skinner, B. F. *Walden two.* New York: Macmillan, 1948.

Skinner, B. F. How to teach animals. *Sci. Amer.,* 1951, **185** (6), 26–29.

Skinner, B. F. *Science and human behavior.* New York: Macmillan, 1953.

Skinner, B. F. The science of learning and the art of teaching. *Harv. educ. Rev.,* 1954, **24,** 86–97.

Skinner, B. F. A case history in scientific method. In Koch, S. (ed.),

Psychology: A study of a science. Vol. 2. New York: McGraw-Hill, 1959.

Sokolov, Y. N. *Perception and the conditioned reflex* (translated by S. W. Waydenfeld). New York: Pergamon, 1963.

Solomon, R. L. Punishment. *Amer. Psychologist,* 1964, **19,** 239–254.

Solomon, R. L., Kamin, L. J., and Wynne, L. C. Traumatic avoidance learning: The outcome of several extinction procedures with dogs. *J. abnorm. soc. Psychol.,* 1953, **48,** 291–302.

Solomon, R. L., and Wynne, L. C. Traumatic avoidance learning: The principles of anxiety conversation and partial irreversibility. *Psychol. Rev.,* 1954, **61,** 353–385.

Wolfe, J. B. Effectiveness of token-rewards for chimpanzees. *Comp. Psychol. Monogr.,* 1936, **12** (60).

Thorndike, E. L. Animal intelligence. An experimental study of the associative processes in animals. *Psychol. Monogr.,* 1898, **2** (8), 1–109.

Thorndike, E. L. *Human learning.* New York: Century, 1931.

Watson, J. B. *Behaviorism.* New York: Norton, 1925.

Wolpe, J., Salter, A., and Reyna, L. J. (eds.) *The conditioning therapies.* New York: Holt, 1964.

Woodworth, R. S. *Experimental psychology.* New York: Holt, 1938.

INDEX

Catalog

If you are interested in a list of fine Paperback
books, covering a wide range of subjects
and interests, send your name and address,
requesting your free catalog, to:

McGraw-Hill Paperbacks
330 West 42nd Street
New York, New York 10036